Passion and Politics
Sir John Lavery: The Salon Revisited

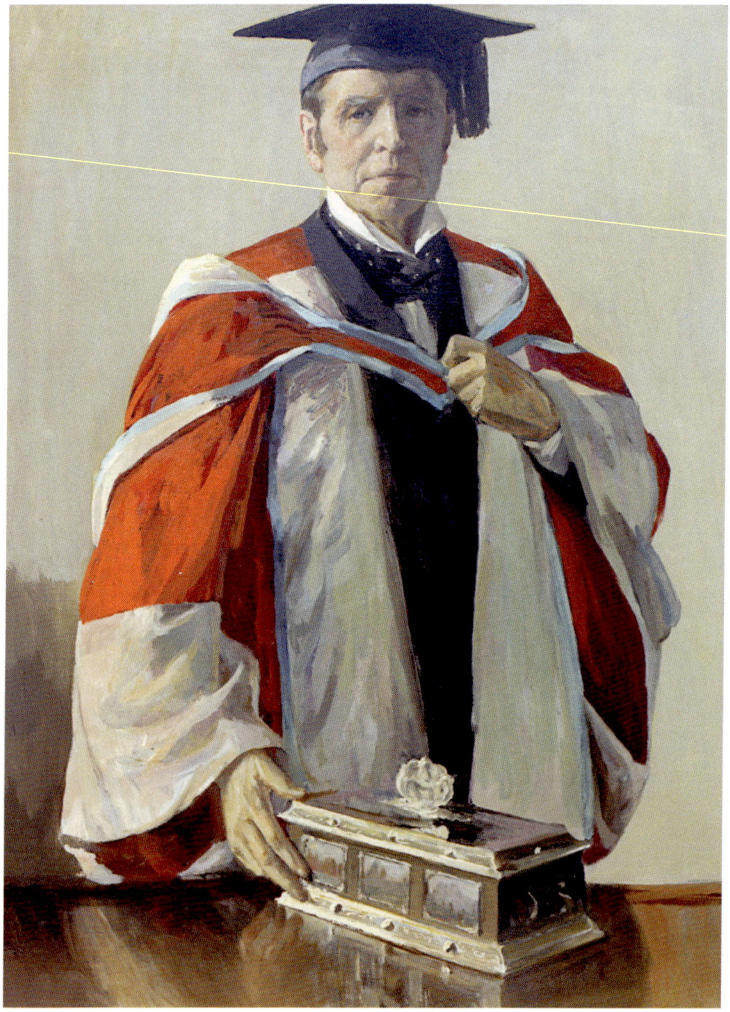

Self-portrait, 1935
Oil on canvas, 101.5 × 76.3 cm (framed)
Collection of Queen's University Belfast

PASSION AND POLITICS

Sir John Lavery: The Salon Revisited

Sinéad McCoole

Dublin City Gallery The Hugh Lane

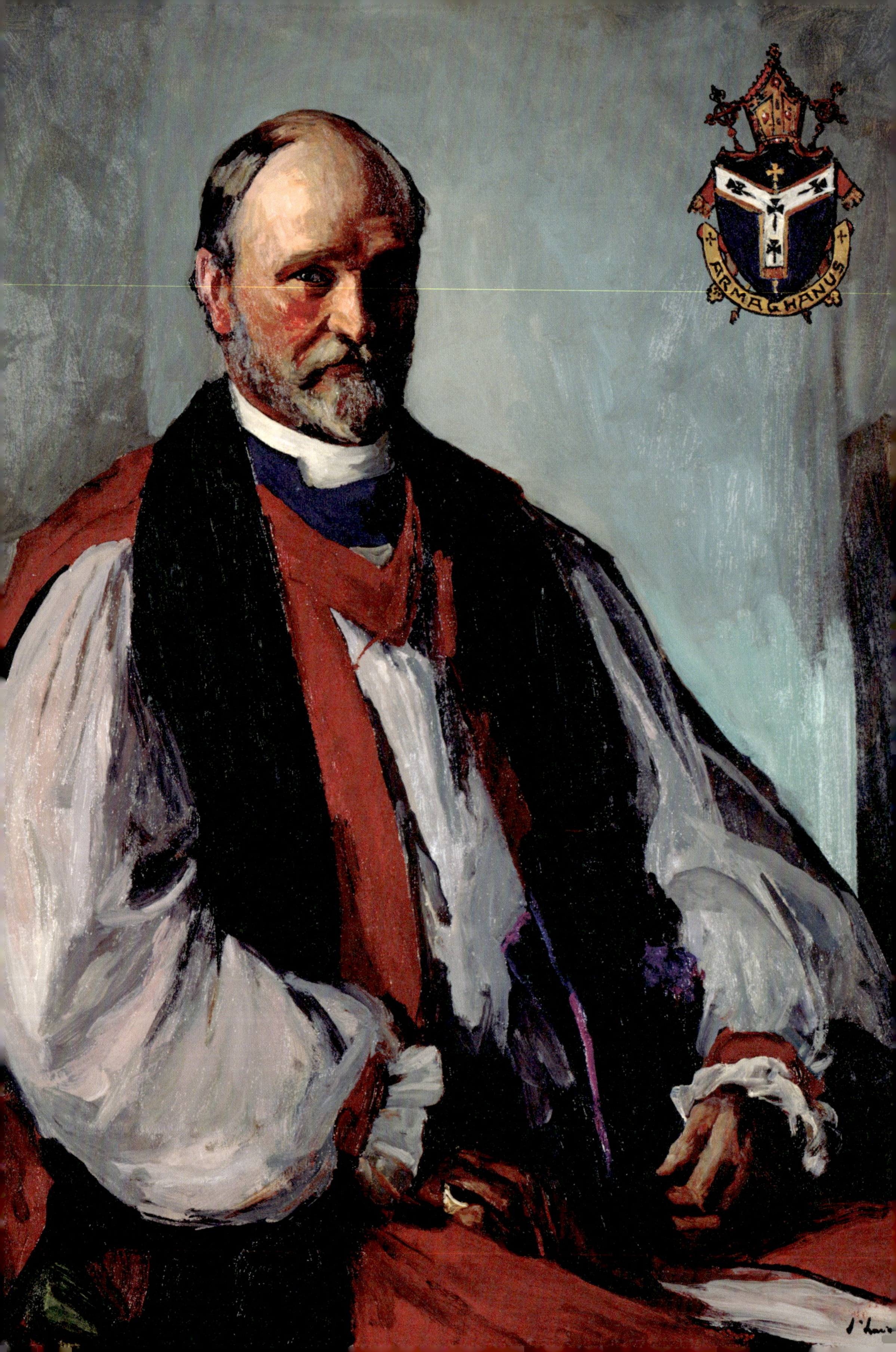
ARMAGHANUS

Contents

Most Rev. Charles Frederick D'Arcy, MA, DD *1859–1938, Archbishop of Armagh and Primate of All Ireland,* 1928
Oil on canvas, 102.1 × 76.3 cm
Ulster Museum

The Cold Heaven[†]

Barbara Dawson
Director, Dublin City Gallery The Hugh Lane

The approach to 2016, the centenary of the Easter Rising, one of the most significant events in modern Irish history, must be seen as the most singular opportunity for a current appraisal of those events which culminated in the birth of modern Ireland as well as a critical evaluation of the consequences for Irish contemporary identity.

At the launch of our centenary in 2008, the acclaimed historian Roy Foster described the establishment of The Municipal Gallery of Modern Art in 1908 as the most important event in Modern Irish Culture. Believed to be the oldest public gallery of modern art in the world, The Hugh Lane has a singular collection of early 20th Irish century art. It is the obvious starting point from which to launch an enquiry into the visual accounts recorded at first hand by artists from that period, beginning with Sir John Lavery.

For an orphan from Belfast who grew up in Scotland, John Lavery's rise to prominence was quite a journey from rags to fame and wealth. From the beginning Lavery demonstrated a steadfast determination to succeed as an artist. Over time he steadily carved out a position as a renowned portrait painter. An academician

† This is taken from the title of a poem by W.B. Yeats, 'The Cold Heaven', first published 1912.

Joseph MacRory, DD 1861–1945, Archiepisciopus Armachanus Totius Hiberniae Primus, 1928
Oil on canvas, 102.2 × 76.5 cm
Ulster Museum

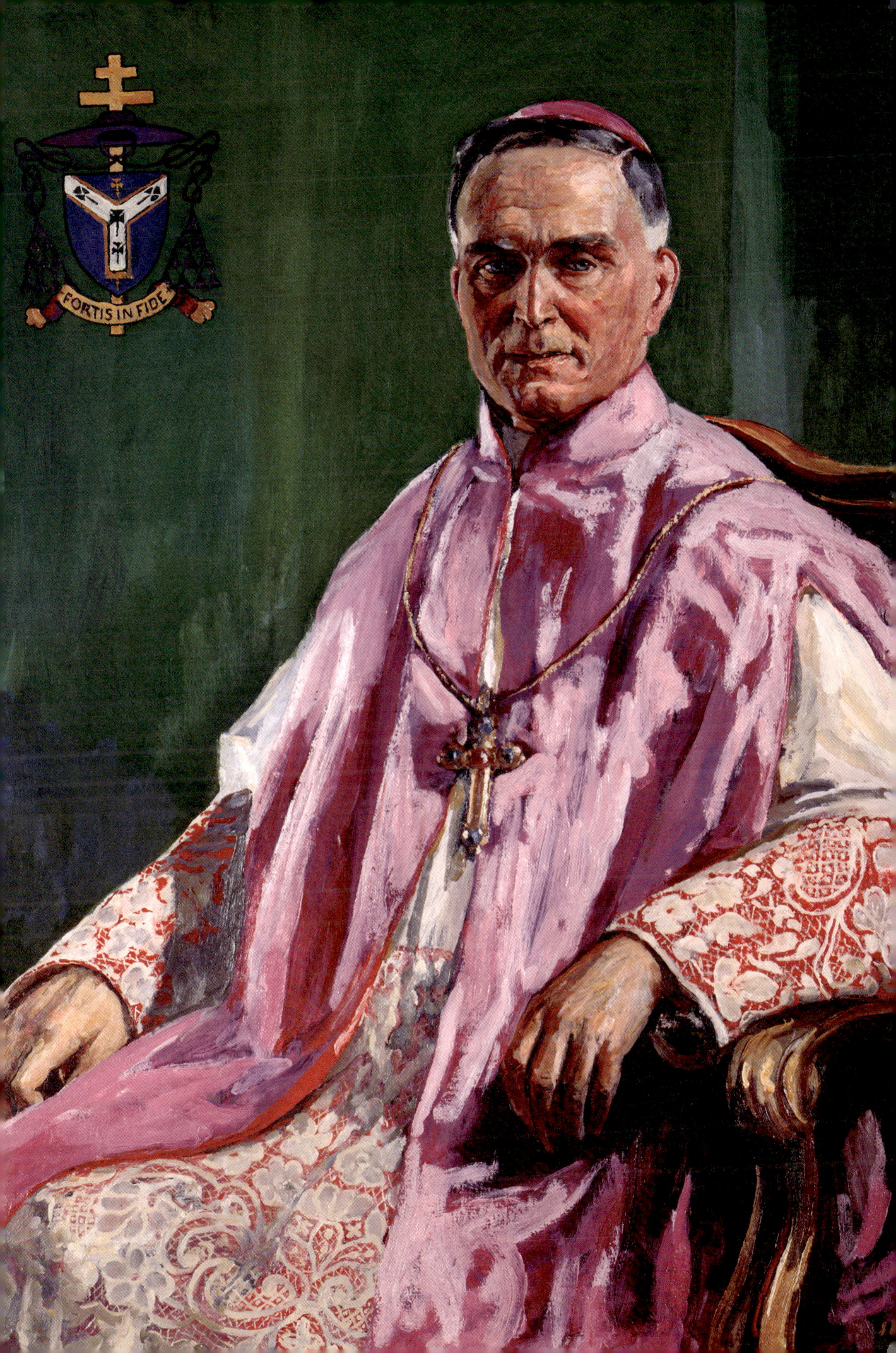
FORTIS IN FIDE

of note, he was a member not only of the Royal Academy, but also of The Royal Hibernian Academy, The Royal Scottish Academy, and the Royal Academies of Rome, Antwerp, Milan, Brussels and Stockholm. In 1910 he was selected for a solo exhibition at the Venice Biennale.

His first important break was a commission from the executive council of the Glasgow International Exhibition to record the state visit of Queen Victoria in 1888. It took over two years to complete as he arranged individual sittings with the main protagonists including the Queen. Following on the success of this work, Lavery moved to London and began his ascent into British society as one of its most renowned and beloved portrait painters.

In today's parlance Lavery became painter to the stars as he enjoyed wealthy patronage from the British establishment. In his journey to fame he was ably supported by his beautiful American wife Hazel Martyn, a painter and printmaker from Chicago whom he married in 1909. Hazel became a London fashion icon noted for her original and flamboyant style. Photographed for *The Tatler* and *Vogue*, it was Hazel who taught Winston Churchill to paint and helped Lavery to move with ease in aristocratic circles.

They were quite an exceptional couple who saw the advantage of press attention and used it to the full. They contrived a celebrity cult status unprecedented in society of that time and Lavery's portraits and plein air scenes are redolent of the life and politics of the privileged classes.

He also enjoyed Royal patronage and was commissioned by the publisher W.H. Spottiswoode to paint a portrait of the George V and his family, the composition of which he based on *Las Meninas* by Velázquez. Such was the rapport between the artist and his sitters that the Royal family paid a visit to his studio in Kensington which was widely reported in the press with much comment on the 'American ways' of his wife Hazel. Her refreshing and open approach was found to be most attractive by many and her attitude and exceptionally good looks greatly helped Lavery with his career.

Despite their friendships and associations with the British establishment neither Hazel nor John were deterred from involvement in Irish politics. One of his earliest forays into Irish political life was when he painted the portraits of Sir Edward Carson and John Redmond, the Unionist and Nationalist leaders, who sat for him in 1916. Redmond remarked that he 'always had an idea that Carson and I might someday be hanged side-by-side in Dublin'. Also from 1916 is his documentation of one of the great miscarriages of justice from that time – the execution of Sir Roger Casement, a former British diplomat. Lavery was granted permission to attend and paint the Court of Criminal Appeal where Casement appealed against his sentencing for treason. In support of the Easter Rising he had attempted but failed to bring arms from Germany. He was arrested immediately upon his return to Ireland and his trial caused a storm.

Lavery's decision to paint Casement sympathetically as he sat in the dock was an extremely brave undertaking for an artist whose livelihood was derived primarily from those opposed to political change. The making of this historical record, which was not commissioned, was widely criticised in the English press with many expressing disbelief that Lavery would concern himself with this highly contentious trial. However he persevered, and as well as several sketches of the Appeal, he finally completed a monumental canvas measuring approximately 2 × 3 metres, portraying all of the key protagonists including Chief Justice Charles Darling who presided over the Court, and the supporters and family of Casement. A unique record of a famous event, Lavery in his will bequeathed the work to the National Portrait Gallery, London. As he suspected it was declined. His second choice was the Royal Courts of Justice, who have since given it on long term loan to the Kings Inn's, Dublin.

During the War of Independence Lavery, encouraged by Hazel, undertook to paint the portraits of the Irish and British negotiators of the Irish Treaty. He also painted a splendidly theatrical account of the Ratification of the Irish Treaty in the House of Lords in 1921, and the tragic figure of Michael Collins lying in state after his murder in Cork during the Civil War. He continued to pay attention to Northern Ireland and painted both Unionists and Republicans there alongside prominent clergy men, both Catholic and Protestant, including the Archbishops of Armagh. He also painted the first Speaker of the House of Commons of Northern Ireland, The Rt. Hon. Hugh O'Neill, and The Most Hon. The Marquis of Dufferin and Ava, First Speaker of the Senate of Northern Ireland. That the Laverys' involvement with both Republicans and Unionists did not undermine either their position or their friendships reveals affable personalities and intelligence on their part coupled with Lavery's steely resolve to complete what he had set out to do, namely recount his country's history as it unfolded through the turbulent decades of the beginning of the 20th century. Earlier in his career at the same time as attempting to enlist in the First World War, he also set up a fund for the widows and families of those executed after the 1916 Rising.

One of his most enduring images in portraiture was Hazel. Her portrait as Kathleen Ni Houlihan (the personification of Ireland in mythology) in 1927 was one of his greatest successes. To their absolute delight his American wife's image was embraced as the face of new Ireland and adorned the State's banknotes. Lavery had created an emblematic and enduring image of a new departure in the country's history.

Following on Hugh Lane's gift of artworks to Dublin in 1908 and his premature death aboard the torpedoed cruise liner *The Lusitania* in 1915, a huge controversy arose over his conditional gift of continental pictures. He had first willed them to the National Gallery, London, and a year and five months later he revoked this decision by writing a codicil to the will which was not witnessed.[‡] John Lavery was among those who championed the return of the paintings to Dublin and in 1935 donated a large collection of his works in memory of his famous wife Hazel Lavery. They were to hang in the room left vacant for the return of Hugh Lane's disputed pictures. He had previously made a considerable gift of works to the then Belfast Museum and Art Gallery, now the Ulster Museum. His gift to the two cities, Dublin and Belfast, the city of his birth, is a significant and invaluable historical record of one of the most turbulent periods in Irish history. Reflecting on this, when W.B. Yeats visited the Gallery in 1938 and saw Lavery's gift, he was moved to write his account of what he too had witnessed in the early decades of the 20th century in Ireland in his much loved poem 'The Municipal Gallery Revisited'.

From the 1916 Rising to the War of Independence through to the birth of the Irish Free State and the State of Northern Ireland; his portraits and paintings are a non-erasable and vivid account of the nascent States. We are both delighted and privileged to bring together for the first time Lavery's generous gifts to Belfast and Dublin. It is a significant and timely exhibition which underpins how influential and pre-eminent our art and artists are in shaping the history of this island. We are extremely grateful to Sinéad McCoole, guest curator, for her illuminating text on Sir John and Lady Lavery and the part they played in early 20th century Irish history.

‡ See *Hugh Lane: Founder of a Gallery of Modern Art for Ireland*, Scala, London, 2008, and *Images and Insights*, Hugh Lane Municipal Gallery of Modern Art, Dublin, 1996.

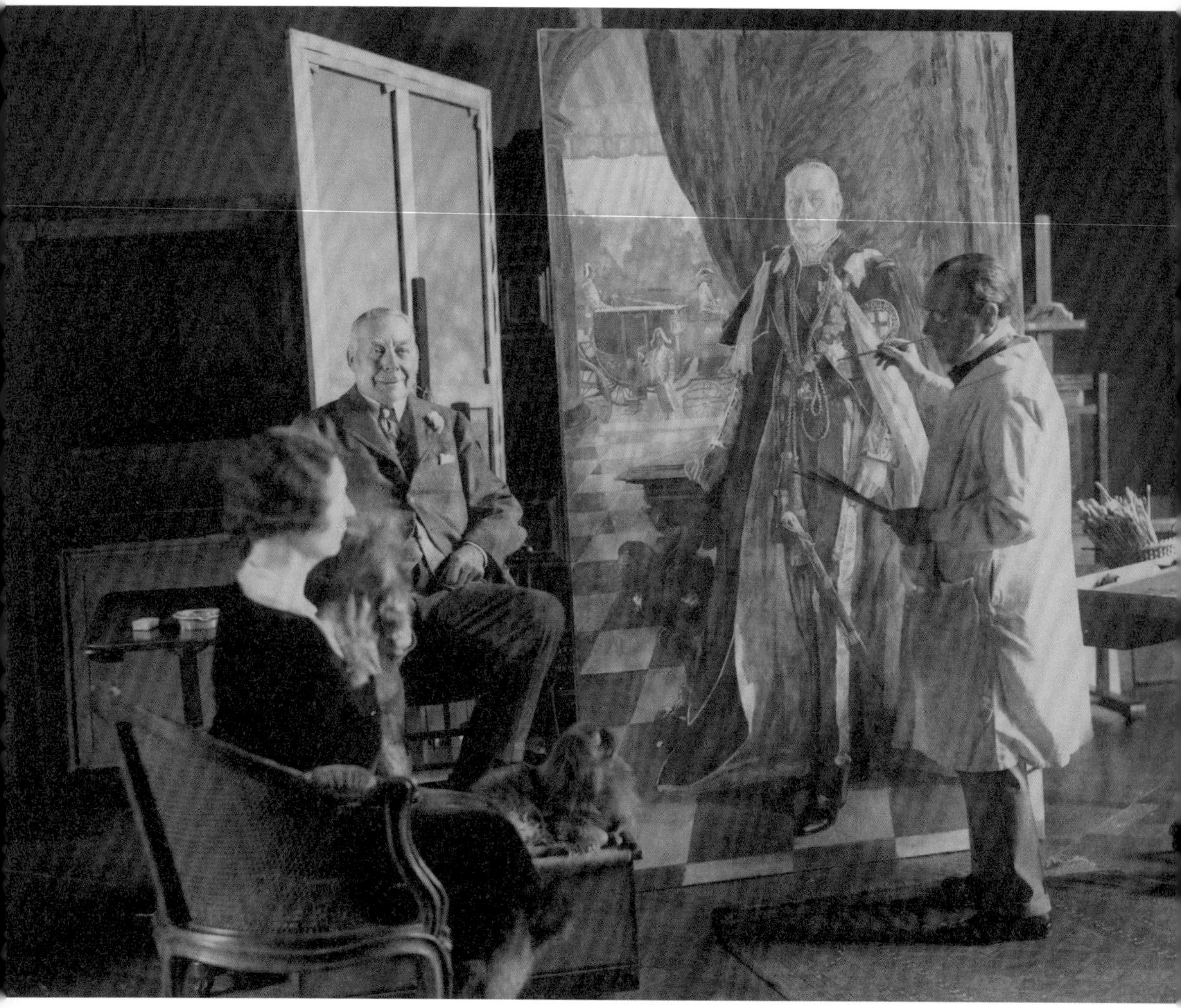

Sir John Lavery painting Lord Lonsdale (1857–1944)
as Lady Lavery looks on, March 1931

Fox Photos / Getty Images

Passion and Politics: The Salon Revisited

Sinéad McCoole

Even before his death, the artist Sir John Lavery had systematically created his own legacy, ensuring his place in Irish history by presenting a selection of his works to galleries in two cities in Ireland, Dublin and Belfast. This self-made man showed remarkable generosity and self-confidence by donating sixty-three of his paintings to the Irish people during his own lifetime. These donated works had not been commissioned. It would therefore appear that they had been created by the artist with the sole intention of giving them into public ownership in the land of his birth. Lavery's portraits of key personages in contemporary Irish life became the first visual representations of the newly shaped Ireland, the partitioned Ireland, which had only just been formalised at the time of his gift, as a result of the Government of Ireland Act 1920, the Anglo-Irish Treaty of 1921 and the Irish Free State Act of 1922, which created a physical border that emerged during the 1920s.

In 1929, the newly opened Belfast Museum (now the Ulster Museum) was delighted by the donation from one of their own.[1] Arthur Deane, Curator, wrote in July 1929: 'Belfast is fortunate in possessing such a collection and proud of such a benefactor'.[2] The collection consisted mainly of portraits of key figures in the life of

1 Although born in Belfast, John Lavery spent only part of his childhood in Ireland. Orphaned at the age of three, he was living with relatives in Scotland by the age of ten. He lived briefly in County Antrim in his late teens and in 1879 he spent a short time giving painting lessons in Belmullet in County Mayo, where he witnessed the terrible poverty of the people of the region. He spent his final months living with his stepdaughter Alice in County Kilkenny, where he died in 1941.

2 Arthur Deane, *Sir John Lavery Collection of Paintings*, Museum and Art Gallery, Belfast, 1929 (Dublin City Gallery The Hugh Lane Archive).

Northern Ireland, politicians and clergy, yet, interestingly, Deane does not refer to these portraits in his introduction to the collection catalogue. On being asked the reason for his donation, Sir John Lavery stated that there were two reasons: 'I was born in Belfast, and the other was that they had built a gallery and they had no pictures to put in it'.[3] This simplistic answer was the essence of Lavery, his uncomplicated and non-partisan approach to all he encountered during his lifetime. Such an approach seemed to allow him to take on controversial subject matter and take part in a host of seemingly contradictory activities such as supporting the widows and dependants of the 1916 Rising, while enlisting in the First World War (he was the Royal Navy's official painter) and later accepting a knighthood for his work as a war artist. He depicted those active in the Irish War of Independence including painting the scene of the London requiem mass for hunger-striker Terence MacSwiney in 1920, while hostilities in Ireland were still ongoing. Lavery then opened his studio in London as an informal negotiation centre during the Anglo-Irish Treaty and its aftermath. He gave credit to his second wife Hazel for instigating his involvement in Irish politics, but this posthumous accreditation of his wife[4] distorts the truth; throughout their marriage they worked together in the creation and maintenance of their lifestyle when their social status, religion and nationality could have meant exclusion. Politics was no exception. Lavery was considered for the role of Governor General, the representative of the British monarch in Ireland in the 1920s. In 1927 he was given the commission, without it being open to public competition, to create the image for the new Irish Free State banknotes. He selected his muse Hazel and for almost seventy years his wife personified an Irish cailín and graced the Irish currency (although her Irish antecedents had left Ireland in the seventeenth century). Lavery always maintained, although there is evidence to suggest otherwise, that he was given the commission because of his diplomatic work on behalf of the Irish during the Treaty negotiations.

3 'Sir John Lavery – His Works a Record of Modern Life,' *Sunday Times*, c.1930, Lady Lavery Scrapbooks (private collection).

4 John Lavery, *The Life of a Painter*, London, 1940. This autobiography was written when Lavery was in his eighties. In it he wished to enshrine Hazel's memory, since her reputation had been tarnished, in particular in Ireland. 'Neither in paint nor in words do I feel I could ever do justice to Hazel … so upon the things nearest to me I will write least.' Lavery, *Life*. p.198.

In the late 1920s, despite his best diplomatic efforts,[5] the gift of a collection of his works to the National Gallery of Ireland in the newly formed Irish Free State was thwarted by the fact that the Gallery's acquisition policy prevented them from accepting images of living persons. Many of Lavery's canvases depicted politicians who were still living. Ireland's recent civil war complicated matters further. The collection included *Michael Collins (Love of Ireland)*, in which Michael Collins is depicted in death, draped with the Irish tricolour.

The collection was finally presented to the Municipal Gallery of Modern Art in Dublin in memory of Hazel, Lady Lavery in 1935. It included the painting *'It is finished'. 5th January 1935 (Lady Lavery)*, a work showing Hazel's coffin in her bedroom. This painting, when seen by this author for the first time as a History of Art student at University College Dublin, realised a curiosity so great that it culminated in her thesis on the Laverys and their role in the foundation of the Irish Free State and subsequently a biography: *Hazel: A Life of Lady Lavery (1880–1935)*, which was first published in 1996 in conjunction with the Hugh Lane Municipal Gallery of Modern Art.

By producing such an extensive visual record, Lavery ensured that the participation of his wife and himself in the making of modern Irish history was fully documented. This visual documentary of their lives would lead to the discovery of Hazel's own records – her scrapbook[6] collection and her letters from the literary, artistic, and political elite of her day. Yet this was solely a collection of their public life. Fleeting references to the deeper story were in the footnotes, the references in memoir, fashion magazines, on film, in novels and in the lines of poetry. This exhibition and catalogue further critically examine the story of the Laverys. On visiting the Municipal Gallery (now Dublin City Gallery The Hugh Lane) in 1937, William Butler Yeats wrote of the Lavery bequest in his poem 'The Municipal Gallery Revisited':

5 Lavery offered the paintings to 'the nation' and tried to work out 'complications' through an intermediary, Thomas Bodkin, Director of the National Gallery. It was the belief of Lavery and the Director that the National Gallery was 'the proper place in which to house them'. Thomas Bodkin to W.T. Cosgrave, Department of the President, 28 September 1929 (The National Archives of Ireland).

6 Lady Lavery's scrapbook collection is in a private collection in Ireland. In the 1970s scrapbooks compiled by Lady Lavery were sold at auction in England. These remain untraced.

I

'Around me the images of thirty years: An ambush (...)
Casement upon trial, half hidden by the bars,
Guarded; Griffith staring in hysterical pride;
Kevin O'Higgins' countenance that wears
A gentle questioning look that cannot hide
A soul incapable of remorse or rest;
A revolutionary soldier kneeling to be blessed;

II

An Abbot or Archbishop with an upraised hand
Blessing the Tricolour. 'This is not,' I say,
'The dead Ireland of my youth, but an Ireland
The poets have imagined, terrible and gay.'

On seeing images of Hazel, Yeats alluded to her own story, much of which he did not know as it had been concealed, and, yet he wrote of her:

Hazel Lavery living and dying, that tale
As though some ballad-singer had sung it all (...)

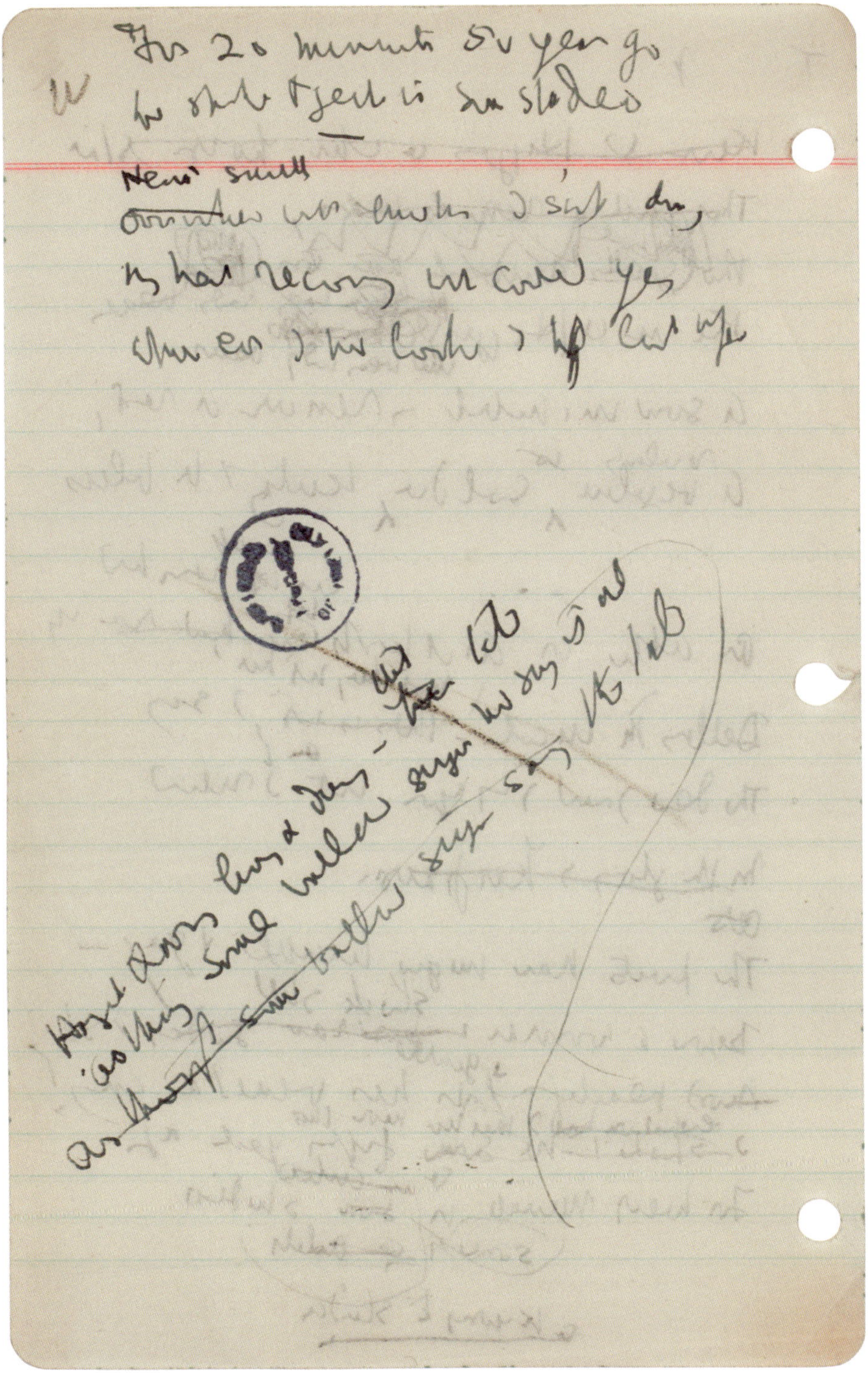

W.B. Yeats: Manuscript of 'The Municipal Gallery Revisited'

National Library of Ireland, MS 13,593 (29) U

John Lavery was born in Belfast in 1856[7] but by the age of three he was orphaned and living with relatives, at first with his father's brother in County Antrim[8] and then with another relative in Saltcoats in Scotland. He said he was called 'the poor wee orphan' and even when he did not quite understand what it meant he made sure to profit by it.[9] He tried many trades until he decided to become an artist as he admired people who could draw. From the humblest of beginnings he set about getting himself an artist's education. He began as a photographer's assistant in Glasgow, doing the mundane task of retouching photographs. According to Lavery's biographer, Kenneth McConkey: 'With no independent means or family to support his career in its early stages, Lavery was forced to be an opportunist.'[10]

He began his formal training at the Haldane Academy, Glasgow, in 1874. His first paintings date to the late 1870s, when he worked in watercolour. He achieved some early success and went to study at Hetherley's school in London in 1879. In 1881 he attended the Académie Julian in Paris. He visited Grez-sur-Loing, the artists' colony outside Paris where he was influenced by the *plein air* painters. He made significant friendships there, including fellow Irishman Frank O'Meara, who features in Lavery's painting *On the Bridge at Grez*, 1884 (National Gallery of Ireland).[11] He painted the bridge at Grez about ten times, beginning in 1883, and returned to Scotland at the end of 1884. Lavery has often been labelled as a Scottish artist because of his involvement with a group of artists known as the 'Glasgow Boys'. These artists with their new 'French' techniques were not in favour with the establishment so they created their own show that travelled to Germany, Austria, Belgium and later to Spain, France, Italy and later to America. As a result, works by these artists, including Lavery, were purchased by national and municipal collections[12] on the continent and in the US.

In 1888 Lavery took the opportunity of being an 'artist in residence' at the International Exhibition at Glasgow. He made forty paintings of different events,

7 His birth date was unrecorded, but his baptism is recorded as 26 March 1856. In his autobiography he said when asked when he was born he chose St Patrick's Day (17 March) as being an Irishman it was easy to remember. Hazel was also known to have said St Patrick's Day was her birthday too – although she was born on 14 March.

8 Lavery never forgot their kindness and visited his cousin Kate Clenaghan throughout his life. When her son Eddie Clenaghan showed artistic ability Lavery brought him over to London and he lived in Cromwell Place for a period of time during 1909. He was later tragically murdered, aged 46.

9 Sir John Lavery, *The Life of a Painter*, London, 1940, p. 17.

10 Kenneth McConkey, *Sir John Lavery RA 1856–1941*, Ulster Museum, Belfast and the Fine Arts Society, 1984, p. 7.

11 Francis Joseph O'Meara was born in Carlow in 1853. He left for France by the age of 20. He returned to Ireland in 1888 where he died at the age of 35. A number of his works are in Dublin City Gallery The Hugh Lane.

12 *The Bridge at Grez* of 1883 was purchased by the Trustees of the Carnegie Institute at Pittsburgh when it was exhibited there in the 1890s. His *Tennis Party*, which won a gold medal in Munich in 1901, was purchased by the Bavarian Government for the collection of the Neue Pinakothek in Munich. Both works were later sold on. *The Bridge of Grez*, 1883, is now in a private collection. *The Tennis Party* was purchased in 1923 by Sir James Murray and presented to Aberdeen Art Gallery.

and afterwards held a small solo exhibition of these works at Craibe Angus Gallery in Glasgow. It was as a result of this that Lavery received his break-through commission from the Executive Council of the International Exhibition to paint *The State Visit of Queen Victoria to the Glasgow Exhibition, August 1888*. At the actual event, Lavery produced a small canvas in situ on 22 August 1888, but the commission was to produce a large historic painting to hang in a public space. As Lavery described to his first biographer, Walter Shaw Sparrow, he got what he considered 'his chance'. He set about arranging individual sittings with those who occupied the premier positions at the state visit. Some 250 individual portraits were created, including those of Queen Victoria and her grand-daughter Princess Alix, who later became the last Tsarina of Russia.[13] This commission gave Lavery the social connections needed to establish himself as a sought-after portrait painter. The mammoth task of organising this massive ensemble of individual sittings meant that over a two-year period John Lavery travelled all over England, Scotland, Wales, Ireland and Germany. Writing of his life, Lavery described his early ruthless ambition, and how he had to orchestrate events in his personal life to ensure he succeeded.[14]

While working on this commission Lavery met a flower seller[15] in London and asked her to sit for him. Lavery was so taken with this 'Irish beauty' that he asked her to be his model. Within a short time she became pregnant. She was also dying of tuberculosis. In order to make sure that his professional ambitions were not compromised, Lavery entered into an unusual domestic arrangement. William Patrick Whyte,[16] who had befriended Lavery in Paris, urged the flower seller, Kathleen MacDermott, to marry the artist, but there is no official record of this marriage.[17] It was William who took Kathleen to numerous health resorts, and finally lived with her at Kilmacolm, a village near Glasgow, where Lavery visited daily. It was here on 1 November 1891 that Kathleen died some months after giving birth to a baby girl who was named Eileen.[18] It transpired after her death that she

13 Lavery was requested to paint a full size portrait of Princess Alix: 'the Grand Duke expressed a wish that I should return when my large picture was finished in order to do a portrait of the future Empress of Russia. But many things interfered, and that opportunity slipped away from me.' Lavery quoted in Walter Shaw Sparrow, *John Lavery and his Work*, London, 1911, p. 77.

14 Lavery writes in his autobiography of his inaction and reaction to his sister's unhappy marriage and subsequent suicide.

15 It was suggested that George Bernard Shaw's flower seller in *Pygmalion* is based on Lavery's meeting with Kathleen, but there is no documentary evidence to substantiate that Lavery and Shaw met when Shaw was writing this story, although they were friends in later years.

16 A watercolourist exhibiting at the Royal Academy, the Royal Institute of Painters in Watercolour, the Royal Scottish Academy and elsewhere between 1882 and 1905.

17 Lavery describes a ceremony as 'I went through the formula with Joseph Crawhall and Patrick Whyte as witnesses', Lavery, *Life*, p. 68. Kenneth McConkey believes there was no formal marriage. This is confirmed by the registration of Kathleen MacDermott's death certificate where John, the informant, is described as neighbour. I am grateful to Kenneth McConkey and Ian Chant Sempill for these references.

18 Eileen was born in London. Kathleen died in Kilmacolm and was buried overlooking the Kyles of Bute. William Patrick Whyte designed the tombstone.

was called Annie Evans and was a runaway from Cardigan in Wales,[19] using the false name of Kathleen MacDermott.

Following Kathleen's death in 1891, Lavery went to Europe. He spent the next five winters in Germany doing 'portrait seasons'. During the early 1890s he travelled extensively on the continent, often in the company of other artists. He visited Holland, Belgium, Italy and Spain, leaving Eileen in the care of William Patrick Whyte. In 1896 he moved to London. In the English capital he reinvented himself. He was now a successful portrait painter, accepting invitations to the select circles that his status as an artist allowed him. He liked the anonymity the city provided, and would write at the end of his life that: 'nowhere I have lived has had the appeal of London nor its freedom. Cromwell Place has been my home for forty years without my knowing my next door neighbour, and it has a call for me that no other corner of the globe had been able to give'.[20] He said that he had purchased the lease of 5 Cromwell Place in 1898 'in a fit of Irish recklessness'. Although it was not a large house, it was in fashionable South Kensington and the whole of the first floor was a studio with a glass roof[21] and a large window.

Lavery had made a rule 'to hold him aloof from any occupation that would interfere with his painting'[22] but in 1897 the International Congress for contemporary artists, which brought about the creation of a new organisation of artists, made him abandon this. He saw the importance of the wider artistic community in the informal spread of pioneering artistic ideals. Although he stated he was no linguist, he spent time learning French, Italian and German. He became a founder member of the International Society, whose aim was to have 'exhibitions of the finest art of the day'. The group also sought to have 'the non recognition of nationality in art'. They established a new gallery in Knightsbridge, called the 'international gallery'. While James McNeill Whistler became President, Lavery became Vice President of what became known as the International Society of Sculptors, Painters and Gravers.

19 Family papers suggest that her father was James McDermot (MacDermott) and that her mother was Marion Evans. Ian Chant-Sempill, Unpublished manuscript on the Sempill Family.

20 Lavery, *Life*, p. 46.

21 The house no longer has the glass roof.

22 Obituary, 1941, Scrapbook belonging to Alice McEnery (private collection).

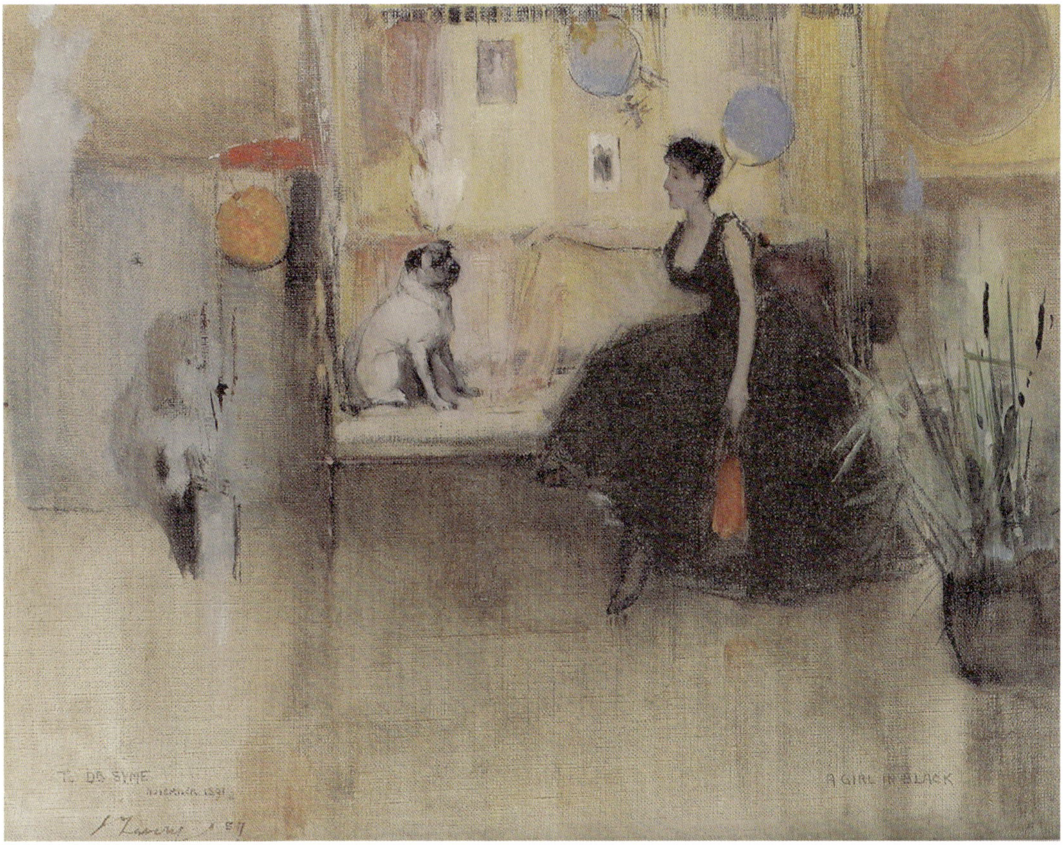

A Girl in Black, 1889
Oil on canvas, 35.5 × 45.7 cm
This is thought to be is a portrait of Kathleen MacDermott. The painting is dedicated 'To Dr Syme / November 1891'. Dr Syme was the general practitioner who attended Kathleen at the time of her death in 1891.
Private collection

Lavery's reputation on the continent grew and in 1901 he was awarded the Cavaliere of the Crown of Italy; in 1907 he was awarded the Chevalier of the Order of Leopold in Belgium. Lavery was aware of the importance of these honours and associations for patronage and exhibition opportunities. He also became a member of numerous societies, including the Royal Scottish Academy (1896) and the Royal Hibernian Academy in Dublin (1906). By 1910, at the height of his powers, a retrospective exhibition of fifty-three of his works was held at the Venice Biennale. 'Although Renoir was also fully represented the daily crowd of Italians who filled the Lavery Gallery was the talk of Venice.'[23]

Lavery was contacted by the Uffizi Gallery in Florence,[24] and invited to paint a self-portrait 'to be hung among the masters'. He later wrote: 'Naturally I was anxious to hand down to posterity all my good qualities, and so I took two years over it, scrapping one attempt after another. Finally I sent it off, and my friends who saw it in the Gallery wrote and told me that I could not be as ordinary as the man who comes to tune the piano or wind the clocks, that I had to give more distinction than I had given myself'.[25] *Self-portrait*, 1909 (Rothe House, Kilkenny)[26] is of a man wearing a plain white coat with no background details; it has no suggestion of his profession as an artist, nor his personal trappings of wealth or status. It is an excellent likeness of John Lavery. In many ways it was a good representation of a man without roots, containing no complex or distracting details.[27]

The following year, perturbed by his friends' comments, Lavery asked for this painting to be returned. As he described: 'I wrote to the Director of the Gallery and made some excuse to get it back. After a couple of months I sent back a new version. There was no comment'.[28] Something of his celebrity status seems to have overcome Lavery's unassuming and easy character, which up to then had brought him so much success. In his new painting he depicts himself as the flamboyant artist. He poses with his hand on his hip, and, although he was just five feet tall, appears large in

23 *Digest*, March 1941. John Lavery Obituaries Scrapbook (private collection).

24 According to Walter Shaw Sparrow, Lavery was contacted by the Italian Government in 1906 to supply a self portrait.

25 Lavery, *Life*, pp. 155–156.

26 This work in Rothe House, Kilkenny, is dated on the verso, 1909. This may be the canvas returned by the Uffizi, as it was always retained by Lavery. It was donated to the Kilkenny Archaeological Society in 1986 by his step-daughter Alice.

27 This self-effacing exploration of self would happen again. His autobiography had the unassuming title *Life of a Painter*. Alice, his step-daughter, disliked the title, saying that it made him seem like a house painter.

28 Ibid.

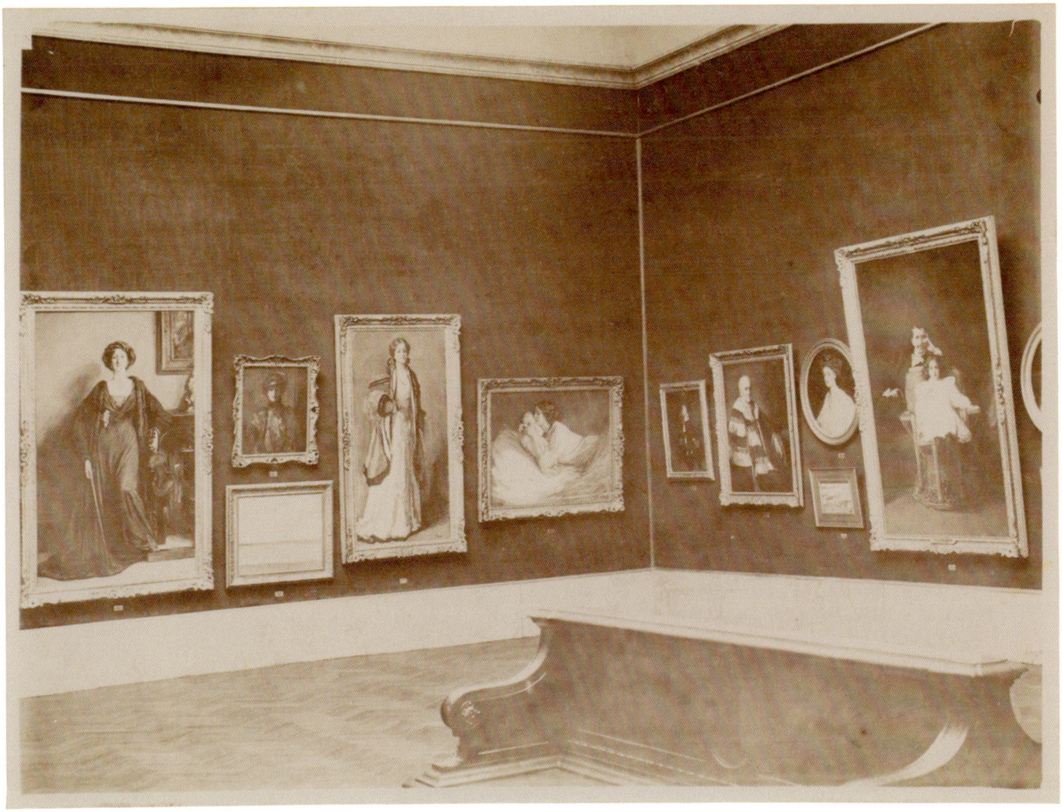

Installation view of John Lavery's room
at the 9th Venice Biennale, 1910
John Lavery Venice exhibition album
Dublin City Gallery The Hugh Lane Archive

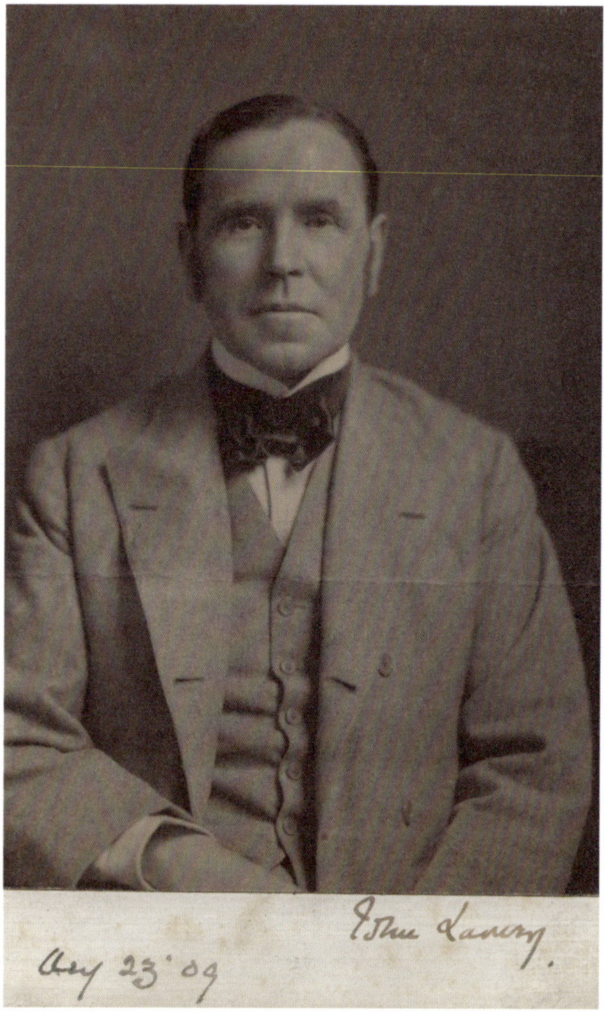

John Lavery, 1909
Platinum print, 15.3 × 10.8 cm (image size)
National Portrait Gallery, London

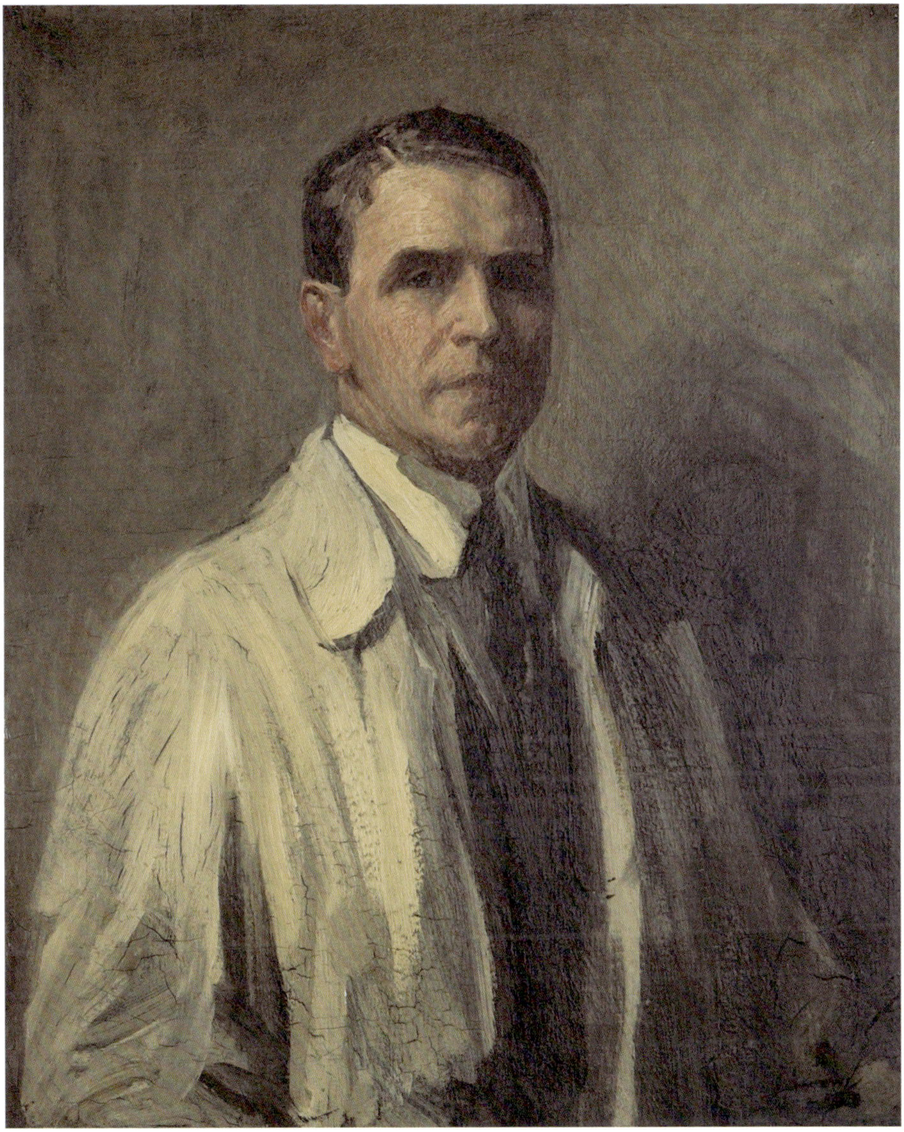

Self-portrait, 1909
Oil on canvas, 68.5 × 61 cm
Kilkenny Archaeological Society, Rothe House, Kilkenny

stature, dominating the canvas. In his hand a dripping paintbrush leaves the viewer in no doubt that this was an artist at work. In the painting he is wearing a necktie, tweed trousers and his white painting coat. Henceforth he would always wear a bow-tie or cravat under his painting coat. It was these details of his appearance that would delight cartoonists throughout his career.

The transformation of his public persona into that of Lavery 'as artist' coincided with his marriage in 1909 to a beautiful woman twenty-four years his junior.[29] Hazel Martyn Trudeau had lived an eventful twenty-nine years by the time she married the fifty-three year old Lavery. Meeting for the first time in France in 1903, they immediately felt a mutual attraction and exchanged self-portrait sketches. Their marriage followed a complicated courtship, spanning a six-year period.

Hazel Martyn met Lavery in the artists' colony Beg-Meil in France in the summer of 1903. She was with her widowed mother and teenage sister Dorothea.[30] The Martyns had arrived in Europe in 1898, and that year had toured on the continent. It is recorded that they travelled to Rome and the French Riviera. Hazel returned to Europe in 1901 and again in 1902, travelling to Paris to study etching, and was tutored in the dry point technique. In spring 1903 she exhibited her work in Chicago. *Chicago Daily News* reported 'men who know pictures are enthusiastic over her work'.[31] The Art Collectors' Club sponsored the publication of her work, *Sketches*. Her work was described as 'the most charming collection of sketches in red chalk and charcoal', which 'delighted the most exacting critics and entirely captured the public'.[32] Like that of many other women artists of the period, her work was described as 'charming'; this too was Lavery's comment on her work.[33] She is said to have responded that she was 'anxious to be taken seriously' and that 'her friends knew nothing of her aspirations to be an artist'.[34] Hazel's mother had indulged her interest in art by taking her to Brittany, a region favoured by the Impressionist and post-Impressionist artists for many years and where many of the villages had artist colonies. A surviving

29 She was born in 1880. All information regarding her age recorded after 1904 is incorrect. Hazel had lied about her age even in official documentation from the time of her first marriage in 1904.

30 Dorothea Hope Martyn (known as Dorothy) was born 17 November 1887.

31 Thomas J. O'Gorman, 'Madonna at a Bullfight', *The World of Hibernia*, vol. 1, no. 1, summer 1995, p. 169.

32 *The Dial*, 1903.

33 John Lavery to Hazel Martyn, undated, October 1903, quoted in McCoole, *Hazel*, p. 14.

34 O'Gorman, 'Madonna', p. 169.

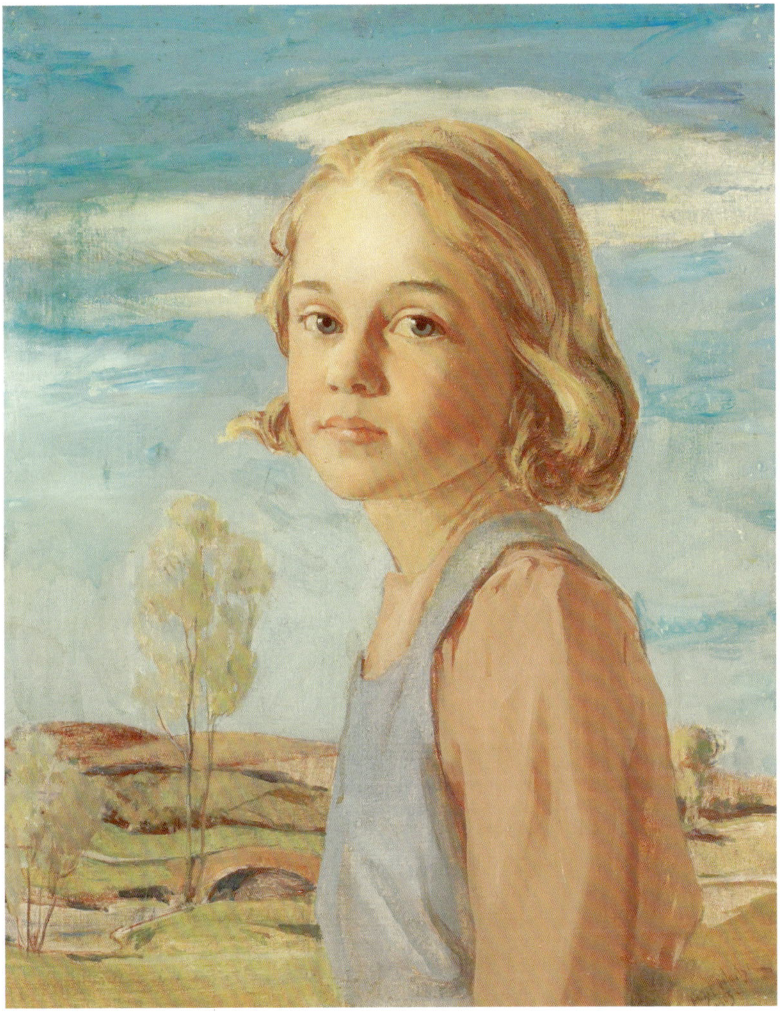

Lady Hazel Lavery (née Martyn):
Portrait of a Young Girl, 1903
Oil on canvas, 51 × 41 cm
Private collection

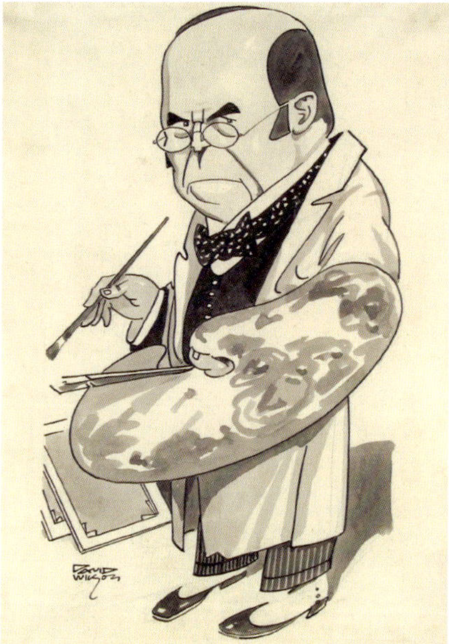

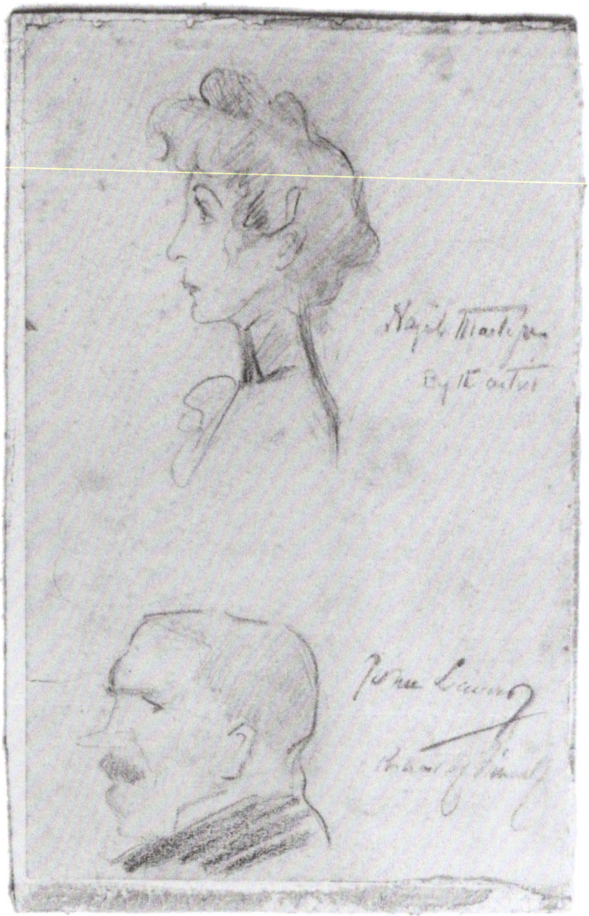

David Wilson: *Sir John Lavery* R.A., c.1912 (detail)
Ink on paper, 35.1 × 26 cm
Collection Dublin City Gallery The Hugh Lane

Self-portrait sketches by Hazel Martyn
and John Lavery, 1903
Private collection

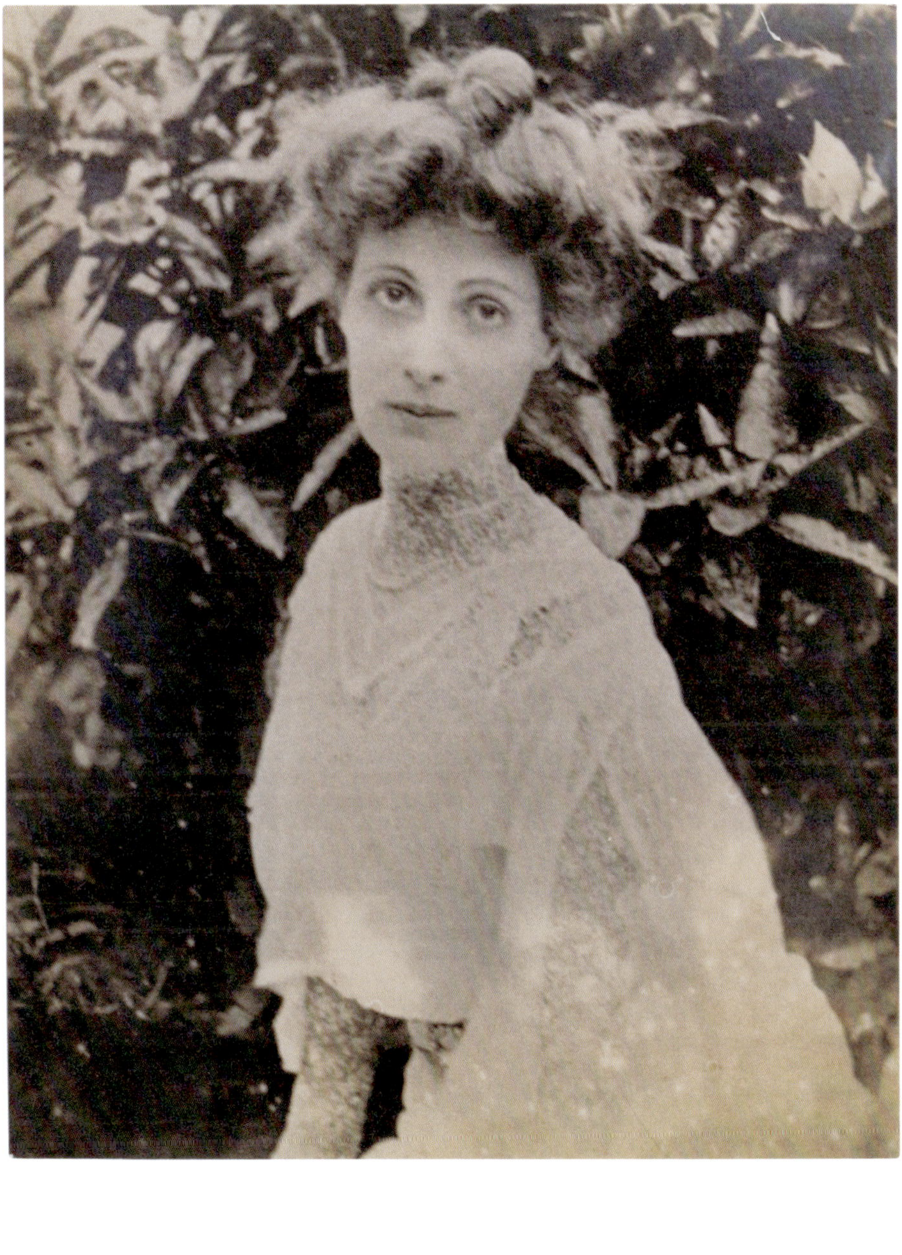

Hazel Martyn Trudeau, 1903

Private collection

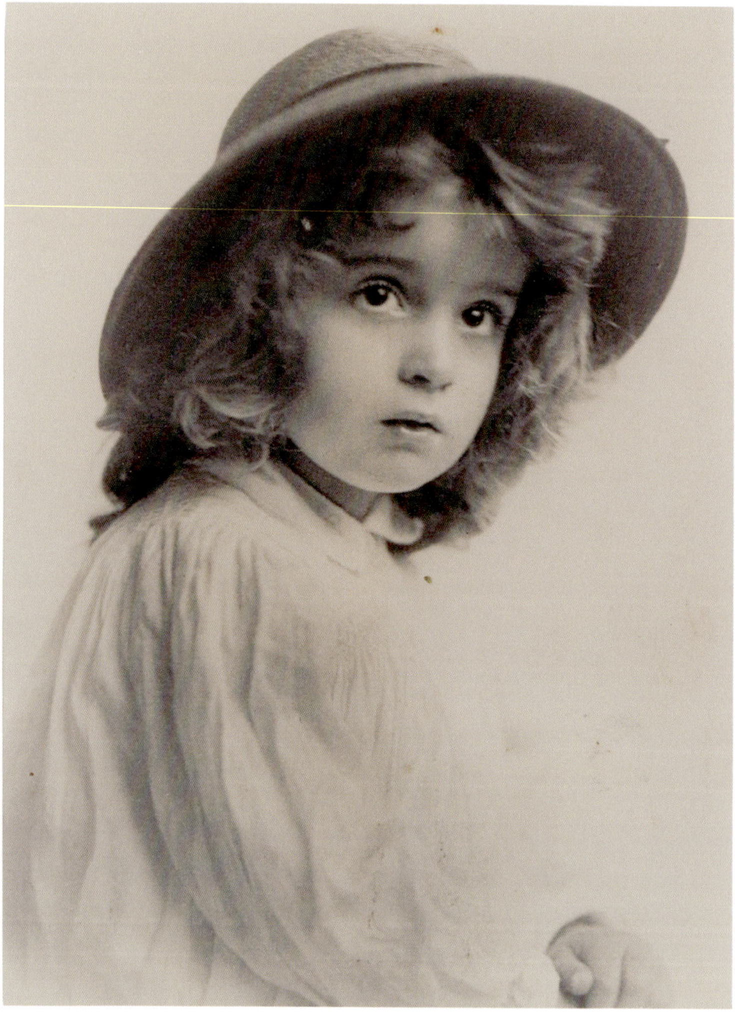

Alice Trudeau as a child, c.1909

Private collection

canvas signed 'Hazel Martyn 1903' shows an unidentified child, a pretty blonde girl, in a rural landscape which is suggestive of France.[35]

Despite the age difference, from the beginning John Lavery and Hazel Martyn were much attracted to each other but this was immediately discouraged by Hazel's mother. Lavery, a widower with a daughter, was travelling with his German model, Mary Auras.[36] Aware of her daughter's interest in this most unsuitable individual, Alice Martyn summoned Hazel's most eligible suitor to come to France. Dr Edward (Ned) Livingston Trudeau, a Yale graduate, was the son of the eminent physician, Dr Edward Livingston Trudeau, Snr, who had pioneered a cure for tuberculosis. Ned went to France immediately, as Dr Trudeau, Snr, described in his autobiography: 'Ned had met in Chicago a Miss Hazel Martyn and had fallen deeply in love with her. She was well known in Chicago and Paris circles as a talented artist and a very beautiful woman. It was love at first sight, and a violent love affair with Ned; and when she went abroad and he left us suddenly, went to Europe, and must have carried the fortress by storm, for he soon returned in the same ship as Miss Martyn and her mother. The marriage took place in Chicago a few months later'.[37] Surviving correspondence between Hazel and John Lavery details how Alice Martyn forced her daughter to marry. Hazel wrote to him on her wedding day that she was marrying against her wishes.[38]

Her ambitions as an artist were undiminished by her marriage. She selected an etching press as her wedding gift in contrast to the usual gift of jewellery.[39] A small studio was set up in their New York City apartment, where Ned and Hazel took up residence in February 1904. The marriage was short-lived, for Hazel was widowed tragically only a few months later. Ned Trudeau was recuperating from pneumonia when, without warning, he died from what was later discovered to be a pulmonary embolism. Hazel was pregnant with their child, a daughter, Alice, who was born the following October. At Hazel's request, Mrs Martyn sent Lavery a telegram a month after the birth. It read: 'Hazel barely lived. Improving. Daughter.'[40]

35 Other surviving works from this period in oils are *Canal in France*, 1904 (private collection) and *The Brown Baby*, 1905 (private collection).

36 Mary Auras later married Nigel d'Albini Black in Morocco and settled there. She accompanied the Laverys on a trip into the interior of Morocco in 1920. She is the model for *Printemps*, 1904 (Musée d'Orsay, Paris). Popular in reproduction, a print of this painting hung for many years in the fictitious home of Vera and Jack Duckworth in the television soap opera *Coronation Street*.

37 Edward Livingston Trudeau, MD, *An Autobiography*, Doubleday, Doran & Company, New York 1915, p. 274.

38 Hazel Martyn to John Lavery, 15 November 1903, quoted in McCoole, *Hazel*, p. 18.

39 'The Lady of the Printing Press', unidentified press cutting, Lady Lavery Scrapbooks (private collection).

40 Telegram from Alice Martyn to John Lavery (private collection).

Hazel returned to live in Chicago were she re-entered society and continued to pursue her art work. In 1905 *Good Housekeeping* magazine selected Hazel as 'one of the well-known artists', reproductions of whose work could be collected by purchasers of 'Armour's Extract of Beef' in exchange for the metal cap from a jar (untraced).[41] Her selection as an artist had much to do with her connections. Her father had worked his way up in Armour's company from messenger boy to Phillip Armour's right hand man. In 1905 Hazel returned for another visit to Europe with her family and continued to paint and to be painted.

In the summer of 1905, while Hazel was visiting the health spa at Malvern Hills in England with her mother, sister and her daughter, Lavery visited her and painted her.[42] The first documented portrait by Lavery of Hazel from this procrastinated courtship is known by the title *Dame en Noir* and also known as *The Brown Furs*, 1906.[43] Hazel had been ill with nephritis, which would account for her ghostly appearance in this painting. It shows her completely wrapped in brown fur, the barely visible gold of the brooch on her fur hat and her necklace supplying the only additional colour. The concentration is on the beautiful but sorrowful sitter. The work was dubbed 'the widow' by Lavery's friend and fellow artist William Patrick Whyte.

Hazel's widowhood did not lead her and Lavery to have an immediate reconciliation and marriage; Mrs Martyn continued to oppose their union, and it was only after her sudden death in London in 1909 that Hazel and Lavery were finally married.

By the time of his marriage, John Lavery lived between Africa and England, spending winters in Morocco. Hazel and Alice accompanied him to Tangiers for the first time in the winter of 1910. He had purchased Dar el Midfah, a small house on the outskirts of the capital. It got its name, 'House of the Cannon', from the fact that there was a cannon half buried in the front garden. Lavery had created a studio with a large flat roof, which was an ideal place to view the city and the sea.

41 The drawings were arranged in six sheets tied with a ribbon ready for hanging. These could be purchased for twenty-five cents or exchanged for the metal cap from a jar of Armour's Extract of Beef.

42 This may be the painting of Hazel in black which was described in Lavery and Hazel's correspondence in 1906.

43 This work was kept by the Laverys. It was used by Temple Thurston as the cover image on his novel *Jane Carroll*, 1927. The story is that of an Irish Republican killed because of his love for a married Englishwoman, Jane Carroll. By giving Thurston the use of this image, public recognition was given to the fact that the heroine of the novel was inspired by Hazel.

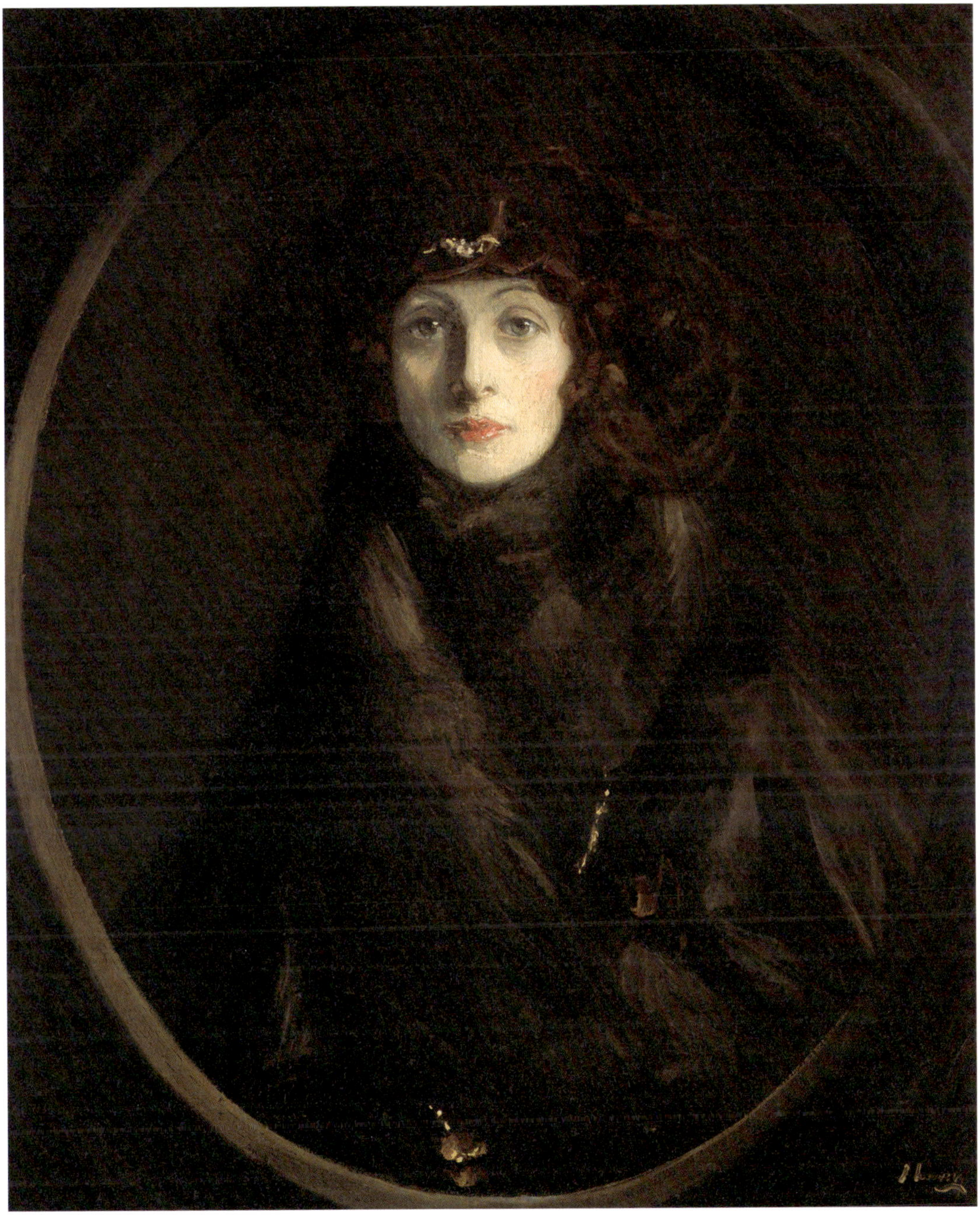

Hazel Lavery (The Brown Furs / Dame en Noir), 1906
Oil on canvas, 77.2 × 64.5 cm
Collection Dublin City Gallery The Hugh Lane

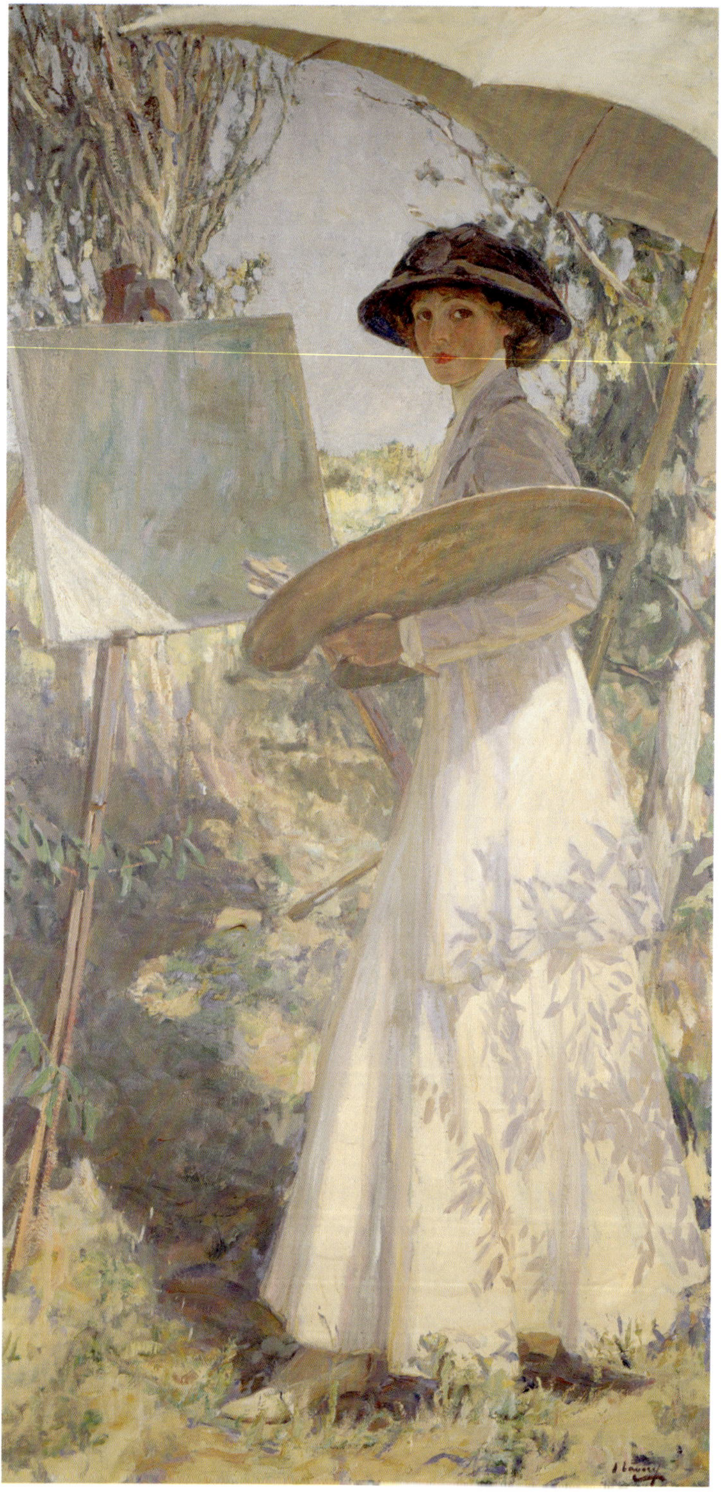

Mrs Lavery Sketching, 1910
Oil on canvas, 203.2 × 99 cm
Collection Dublin City Gallery The Hugh Lane

Mrs Lavery Sketching, 1910,[44] depicts Hazel as the artist, in bright sunlight suggestive of Morocco. Completely different from any portrait Lavery produced of her afterwards, the clothes and setting are secondary here. The fleeting 'impressionistic' moment is paramount; he succeeds in implying that the image was transferred onto the canvas in a matter of minutes.[45] The spontaneity in this portrait is not found in later works. Usually Lavery's method was to produce a smaller sketch before completing a larger work. In this instance the work retains a freshness that has no suggestion of being rigidly reworked.

Mother and Child, 1909, is the earliest known portrait of Lavery's stepdaughter Alice.[46] When it was exhibited the sitters were unknown. Hazel's dark furs and Alice's hat and muff suggest mid-winter and an imminent journey. Similar to *The Brown Furs*, once again the touch of colour is given to the canvas by Hazel's jewellery.[47] The beauty of the mother is conveyed yet there is a deliberate detachment and there is little emotional unity between the mother and child in this picture.[48] Some twelve years before, Lavery had painted a similar composition of himself and his daughter Eileen, *Père et Fille*, c.1900, which was purchased by the French state for the Musée du Luxembourg (now in the Musée d'Orsay, Paris). The painting was admired by James McNeill Whistler when he saw it in Lavery's studio. This formal arrangement of father and daughter seems to have more emotional depth, yet theirs was an unconventional relationship. Eileen spent much of her childhood away from her father. The father figure in her life was William Patrick Whyte, who lived with her and her nurse after her mother's death until they moved to live with Lavery in 1898 when he moved into 5 Cromwell Place, London.[49] By contrast, Lavery immediately had an excellent relationship with Alice, and recalled that the five-year old wanted him to marry her when they met; when he told her he wanted to marry her mother, she said in a resigned voice, 'Well, we'll just have to be friends.'[50]

44 This painting was entitled *Ma Femme* when it was exhibited at the Paris Salon. It has also been known as *Portrait of the Artist's Wife*.

45 In 1905, when she was staying in the Malvern Hills, Hazel wrote that she was painting out of doors. Lavery had given her an umbrella to protect her from 'Father Sol' and a box to carry her canvases, see McCoole, *Hazel*, p.23. Interestingly both these items feature in *Mrs Lavery Sketching*, but the light in this painting suggests a hotter climate.

46 This painting maybe dated earlier. It was described by Alice as 'my mother as a young widow, with me as a child before my step father married her'; see Alice McEnery, 'Sir John Lavery's Kilkenny Connections', unidentified press cutting, scrapbook (private collection).

47 The painting remained in the family possession. It was willed to Alice who donated it to The Hugh Lane Municipal Gallery of Modern Art in 1964.

48 This painting is in complete contrast to his portrait of his daughter and grand-daughter, *Eileen and Ann*, 1923, in which Eileen has a protective arm around her daughter, whose expression is one of total frustration, but completely resigned to pose as requested by both her mother and grandfather. See illustration in Lavery, *Life*.

49 The 1901 census lists the residents at 5 Cromwell Place as John Lavery widower, artist, Eileen Lavery (10 years old) and William Patrick Whyte, artist, is listed as a visitor. I am grateful to Paul Turnell for this reference.

50 Lavery, *Life*, p.131.

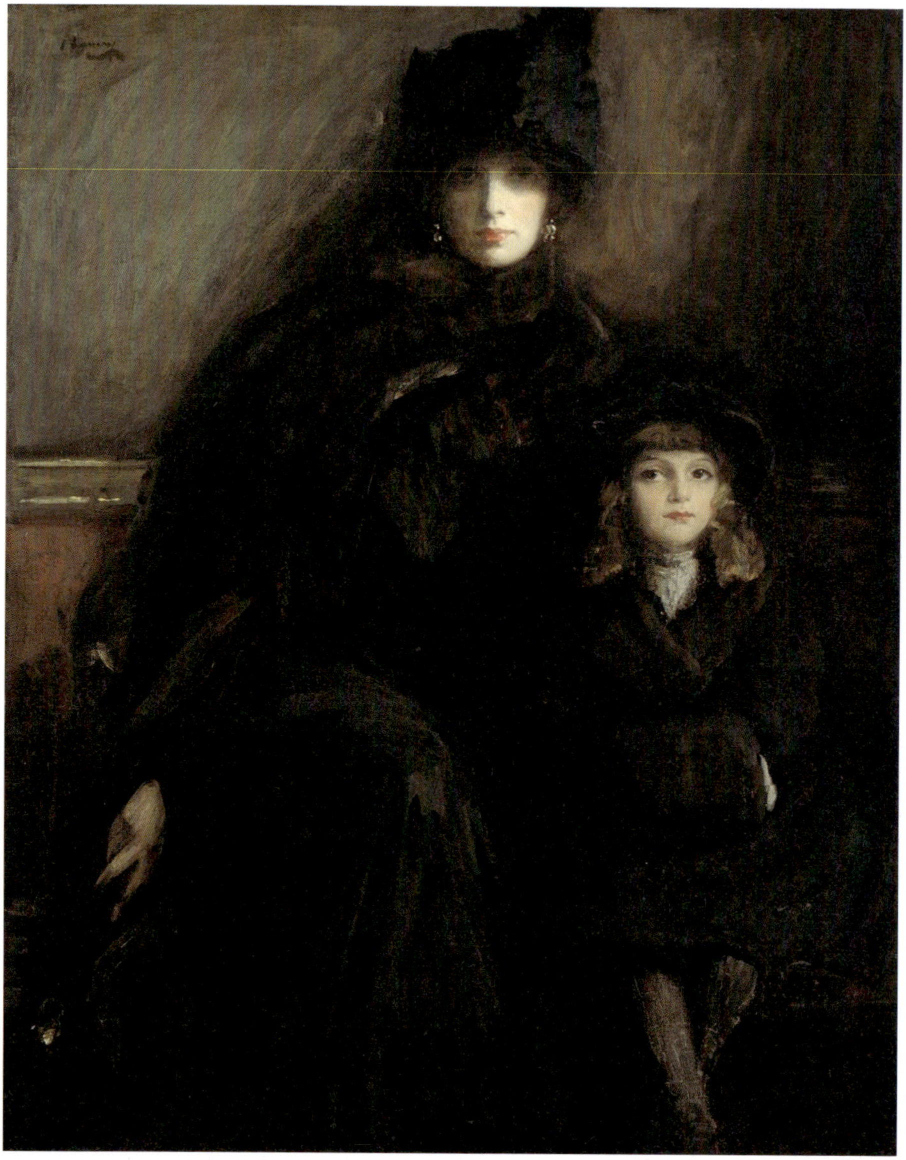

Mother and Child, 1909
Oil on canvas, 124.5 × 100.3 cm
Collection Dublin City Gallery The Hugh Lane

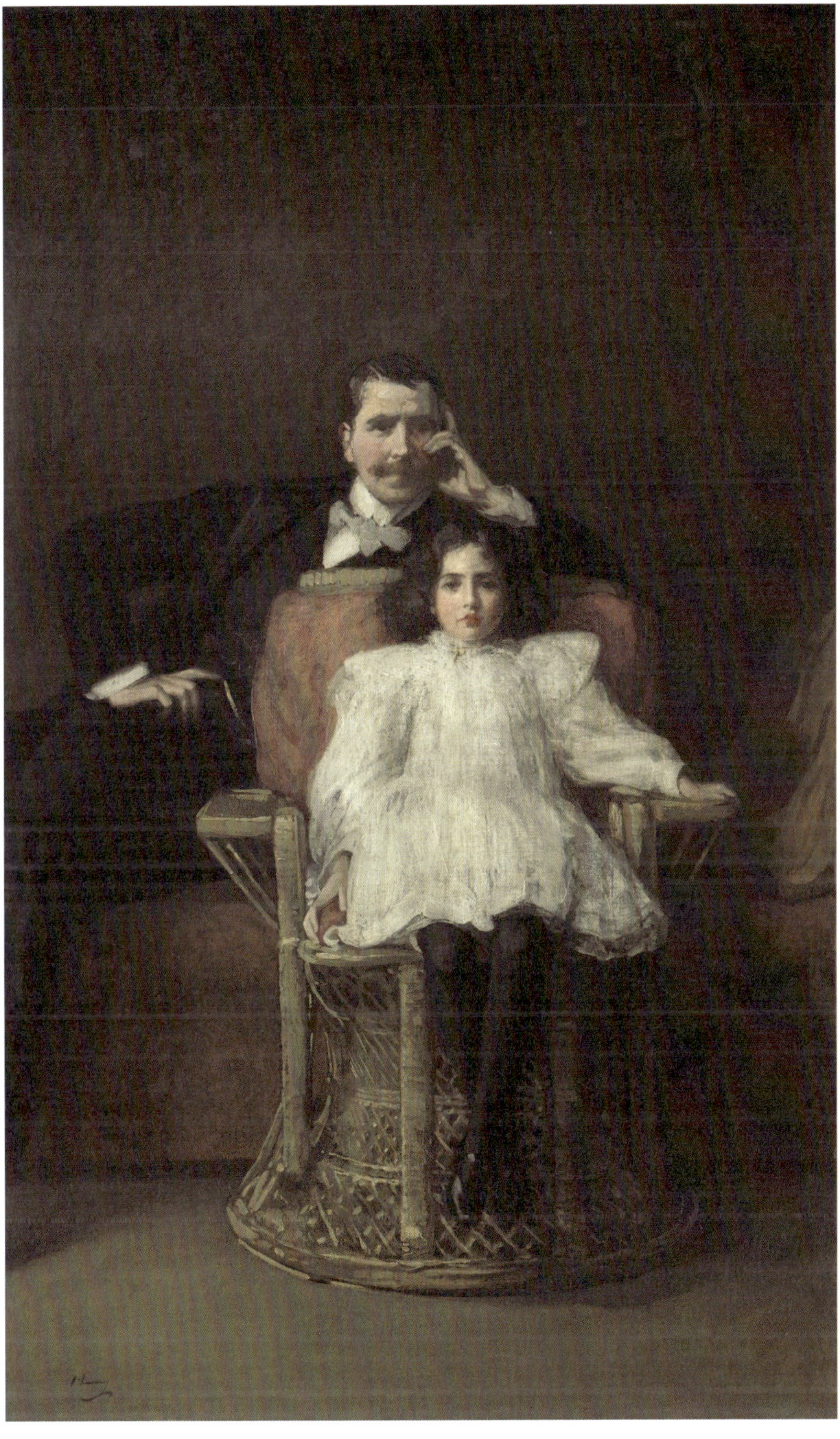

Père et Fille, c. 1900
Oil on canvas, 209 × 126 cm
Musée d'Orsay, Paris

A series of portraits of Hazel was begun and in 1911 Lavery completed a formal portrait of his new wife and his daughter Eileen, both wearing evening dresses. Lavery called this painting by the provocative title *La Belle Mère*.[51] It seems to be a visual manifestation for the artist of his new relationship, placing his own twenty-year old daughter standing behind her stepmother. It is a most unflattering depiction of Eileen. She is dressed in white, while Hazel again is the focus, in particular as she is wearing a blue plume, which immediately draws the viewer's attention to her. Her status is all important.

When Lavery was finally selected to become an Associate of the Royal Academy in 1911, it was naturally a portrait of Hazel that he exhibited. A head and shoulders portrait of her in a colour scheme of gold and silver displayed, as one spectator commented, 'the exquisite harmony… never broken by a single note of definite colour'.[52] The details of the sitter's costume are important – her sable furs, pearls and pendant earrings. The turban, 'a silver gauze adornment', gave the canvas its name[53]: *The Silver Turban*.[54] At the time of exhibition, the sitter was unidentified. One newspaper, under the headline 'The Academy: Society Portraits', wrote: 'Who is the lovely lady who sat for Lavery's *Silver Turban*?'[55] Another stated that the painting was: 'English in character and oriental in surroundings',[56] while a third newspaper wrote: 'Mr. Lavery sends *The Silver Turban*, a picture of a pale-faced and pink-lipped lady who suggests an Eastern atmosphere but who is none the less obviously English. It is a work of rare distinction and refinement'.[57] *The Bystander* described it as 'the most beautiful portrait of the year'.[58]

The Silver Turban marked the formal arrival in society of Mrs John Lavery. Henceforth, the London society columns would mention Hazel on a regular basis and it is from this point on that Hazel began her scrapbook collection. The reason for her anonymity for the previous two years had much to do with her personal circumstances. There certainly had been the creation of a new identity for Hazel,

51 In the probate listing, this painting was left to Alice. It was sold into a private collection by Pyms Gallery, London, in the early 1990s.

52 'Gallery I', unidentified press cutting, Lady Lavery Scrapbooks (private collection).

53 'Royal Academy The May Exhibition Some Notable Pictures', unidentified press cutting, Lady Lavery Scrapbooks (private collection).

54 Purchased by Herr von Meister in 1912; sold by Sotheby's at Gleneagles, Scotland, in 1972; in 1996 believed to be in a private collection in the USA.

55 'The Academy: Society Portraits', Lady Lavery Scrapbooks (private collection).

56 Unidentified press cutting, Lady Lavery Scrapbooks (private collection).

57 Unidentified press cutting, Lady Lavery Scrapbooks (private collection).

58 *The Bystander* (Early Summer and Fashion Number), Undated press cutting, Lady Lavery Scrapbooks (private collection).

for she had actively concealed her past life. Following her marriage, Hazel had returned to America with her mother's ashes. While in Chicago she made the shocking discovery that she was penniless. Her visit was taken up with the sale of the family possessions in order to support her sister Dorothy, who was suffering from ill health and had no form of income.[59] Hazel could retain nothing for herself and wrote in a letter to Lavery from Chicago: 'I am dismantled and impoverished and a beggar child'.[60] Whatever status Hazel once had was gone. She could no longer bring to the marriage her own money and it was therefore imperative that from this point on the couple combine their skills to maintain their position in society. Their sole income was from Lavery's painting. Portraits of Hazel were a systematic creation of an icon; McConkey has described them as 'not just the projection of a lifestyle, but the manufacture of mystique … throughout all, the constant factor is the belle allure of the sitter'.[61]

The Laverys managed to maintain a pre-eminent position by being calculating self-publicists. They knew the importance of being in the fashionable set as well as being able to move freely among all the different groups within society. They numbered among their friends politicians, as well as those who excelled in the world of literature, the arts, sports and business. Before his marriage to Hazel, John Lavery had already demonstrated his ability to move in several social circles, a role that had been highly prized for centuries – the role of the artist diplomat. *The Artist's Studio*, 1910–1911, can be read as an autobiographical statement at a critical moment in the artist's life. This large canvas was reworked by Lavery over a period of three critical years, 1910 to 1913. He reworked and changed it at the time of his important commission to paint King George V and Queen Mary with their family, a work that was to be given into public ownership (now in the collection of the National Portrait Gallery, London). There are a number of similarities in the two canvases, in particular how Lavery arranges the Royal family in a similar grouping to his own family.

59 Her mother had run up huge debts maintaining a lifestyle she could not afford. What monies that remained were inaccessible, as Alice Martyn had rewritten her will in 1905 to ensure that if Hazel died the Trudeau family had no claim to the Martyn estate. The way it was written prevented her own children from obtaining the principal when she died. See McCoole, *Hazel*, p. 39.

60 Hazel Lavery to John Lavery, 11 August 1909, quoted in McCoole, *Hazel*, p. 39.

61 Kenneth McConkey, *The Irish Arts Review*, 1984, p. 16.

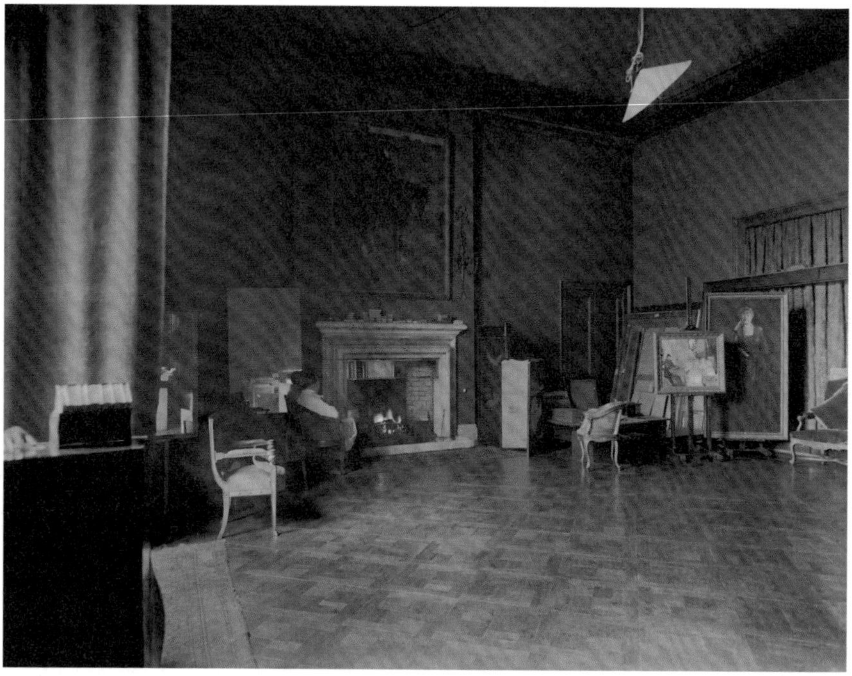

Bassano: *Sir John Lavery in his Studio,*
28 October 1919
Whole-plate glass negative
National Portrait Gallery, London

The Artist's Studio: Lady Hazel Lavery with her Daughter Alice and Stepdaughter Eileen, 1910–1911
Oil on canvas, 344 × 274 cm
Collection, National Gallery of Ireland

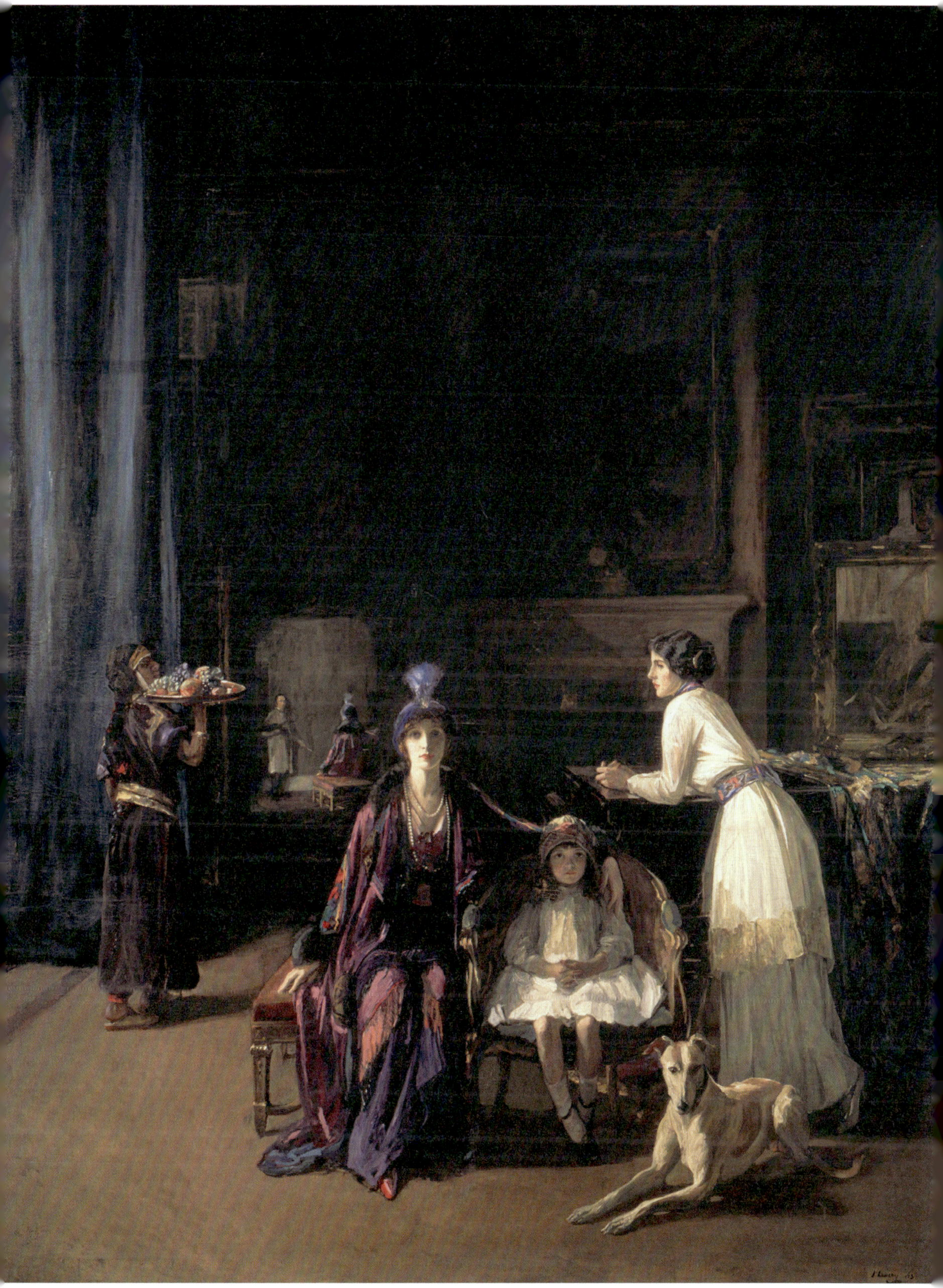

The massive canvas of *The Artist's Studio*[62] was created in homage to Diego Velázquez's *Las Meninas* (The Maids of Honour), 1656 (Museo del Prado, Madrid). The earliest version of Lavery's painting shows the artist in the same position as the Spanish master in the famous painting. This version of *The Artist's Studio* reflected the true nature of the household at 5 Cromwell Place one year after Hazel and her daughter came to live there. It shows the studio crammed with people, Lavery himself standing in the left foreground, paintbrush in hand, while Hazel and Alice sit centrally and Eileen is seated slightly behind on the right. The men featured in the painting must be the constant visitors to Cromwell Place in those years, Lord Alexander Thynne and Lord Ian Blackwood (known as Basil). Both men complained that they could not visit Hazel alone as the other was always there.[63] The other male figure placed slightly closer to the main group is William Patrick Whyte, who had lived in 5 Cromwell Place until Hazel and Alice arrived. He continued to be a regular visitor to the house; guests recalled him in the background 'like a grey ghost, oblivious to them and his surroundings'.[64] Aida, the Moorish maid,[65] is also seen, holding aloft a tea tray; her outfit is suggestive of a formal maid's uniform.

This painting was exhibited in Rome in 1911 but Lavery was unhappy with the composition[66] and took a series of photographs of Alice sitting in different positions and of Aida, posing with a tea service. A preparatory oil painting, *The Studio*, 1911, (now in a private collection) reveals many of the changes seen in the final version of the work: the three male figures have been removed and the impression of a spacious studio is created instead. In this version Lavery does not include himself, but in the finished work, now in the collection of the National Gallery of Ireland, Lavery chooses the same location of the King and Queen in the Spanish master's painting for his mirror image. Hazel's arm around Alice is reminiscent of the earlier *Mother and Child*; once again the pose gives the impression that the show of intimacy is contrived. Eileen is shown wearing an outfit in keeping with her age and status,

62 The painting is now in the National Gallery of Ireland. It was first purchased by Lord Cowdray and exhibited in the great library of his Aberdeenshire home, Dunecht.

63 Both men were to die in the First World War. Lord Basil Blackwood joined the Intelligence Corps and was killed in action on 3 July 1917. Colonel Lord Alexander Thynne was killed commanding the 6th Royal Wiltshire Regiment on 14 September 1918.

64 Morris manuscript, quoted in McCoole, *Hazel*, p. 37.

65 Aisha (who preferred Aida as it sounded Spanish) was smuggled out of Morocco. When it was time for her to return to Morocco she refused saying, 'Me free under British flag'. Aida told a journalist that she was a Moorish princess. Her evidence was a portrait of her that featured in an Italian journal. The caption read: 'Aida, from the collection of His Majesty the King'. This allowed her to make up stories that the Laverys were treating her like a slave. It resulted in an article in *Truth* entitled 'Brown Slave Trade in our Midst.' Like many other women in domestic service, Aida left the Laverys to work in a munitions factory during the First World War. Lavery, *Life*, pp. 131–133.

66 Walter Shaw-Sparrow noted: '*The Studio of the Painter*, c. 1910, 11 ft 6 inch × 9 ft, exhibited at Rome in 1911'. According to Kenneth McConkey, in his examination of *The Artist's Studio* in the National Gallery of Ireland, given the size of the canvas and the pigment on the canvas, it is over-painted.

while, by contrast, Hazel is dressed as if it were another season, in heavy velvet clothes and an elaborate turban. Aida is dressed in Moorish costume and carrying fruit, a reference to the artist's life in Africa. Lavery selected two works to be on display in his studio: *An Equestrian Lady (Idonia in Morocco)*, 1891–1901 (Culture and Sport Glasgow (Museums)) and the portrait sketch of Queen Mary, 1913 (The Royal Collection).

Between February and April 1913, sittings for individual head studies were completed for *The King, the Queen, the Prince of Wales and the Princess Mary, Buckingham Palace*, 1913 (National Portrait Gallery, London).[67] Lavery had been commissioned by Hugh Spottiswoode to paint a group portrait of the Royal family, a work that would be exhibited by the artist before it was donated to the nation.[68] It was the ultimate in society patronage to receive this commission; Lavery had the added cachet of having had access to Buckingham Palace, where the White Drawing Room had been made available to him as a temporary studio.

On 10 April Lavery had the honour of the Royal family visiting the studio. He recorded later how he gave the King the paintbrush to paint the royal blue of the Garter ribbon, writing: 'It is recorded that when Velázquez completed *Las Meninas*, King Philip asked for a brush and colour and painted the Red Cross of the Knights of Calatrava on the breast of the painter in the picture.'[69] The arrival of King George and Queen Mary in South Kensington was reported in the press: 'Now, Mrs. John Lavery is an American, and her child, who so nearly resembles her, has the same transatlantic simplicity and free easiness of manner which one finds so attractive.'[70] The fact that Hazel was American was a huge asset in the rigid formality of the English upper classes, and she used it to her advantage, although, in fact, she had distanced herself from America and her old friends after the death of her sister Dorothy in October 1911. Dorothy had died of anorexia nervosa, an illness which had become more acute in the aftermath of Alice Martyn's death. Hazel had been

67 A sketch was submitted and received the Queen's approval. There are two preparatory oils, with slight arrangement changes, one of which is in the Royal Collection while the other was retained by the artist (now in the Ulster Museum).

68 The Ulster Museum's painting was donated in 1919. According to John Lavery, it was to show that he was not a bigot as he had presented *The Madonna of the Lakes* to St Patrick's Church in Belfast. In his correspondence with the priest at St Patrick's Church he states that he wished newspaper reports of the gift to be issued at the same time.

69 Lavery, *Life*, p. 159.

70 'News and Views – The King and Mr. John Lavery's Little Girl', unidentified press cutting, Lady Lavery Scrapbooks (private collection).

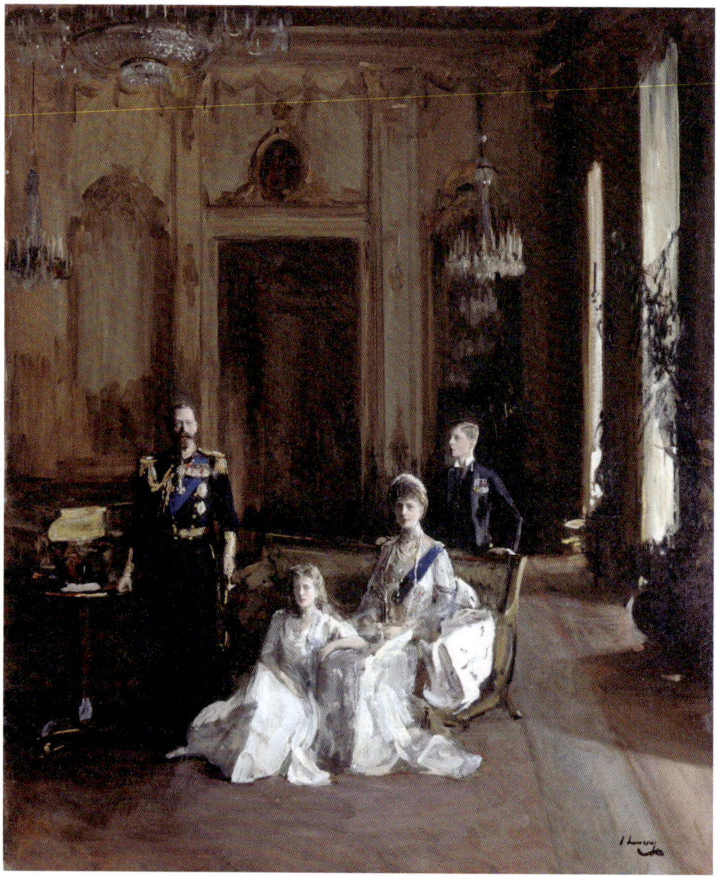

Second Study for the King, the Queen, the Prince of Wales, the Princess Mary, Buckingham Palace, 1913
Oil on canvas, 76.1 × 63.4 cm
Ulster Museum

The King, the Queen, the Prince of Wales and the Princess Mary, Buckingham Palace, 1913
Oil on canvas, 340.3 × 271.8 cm
National Portrait Gallery, London

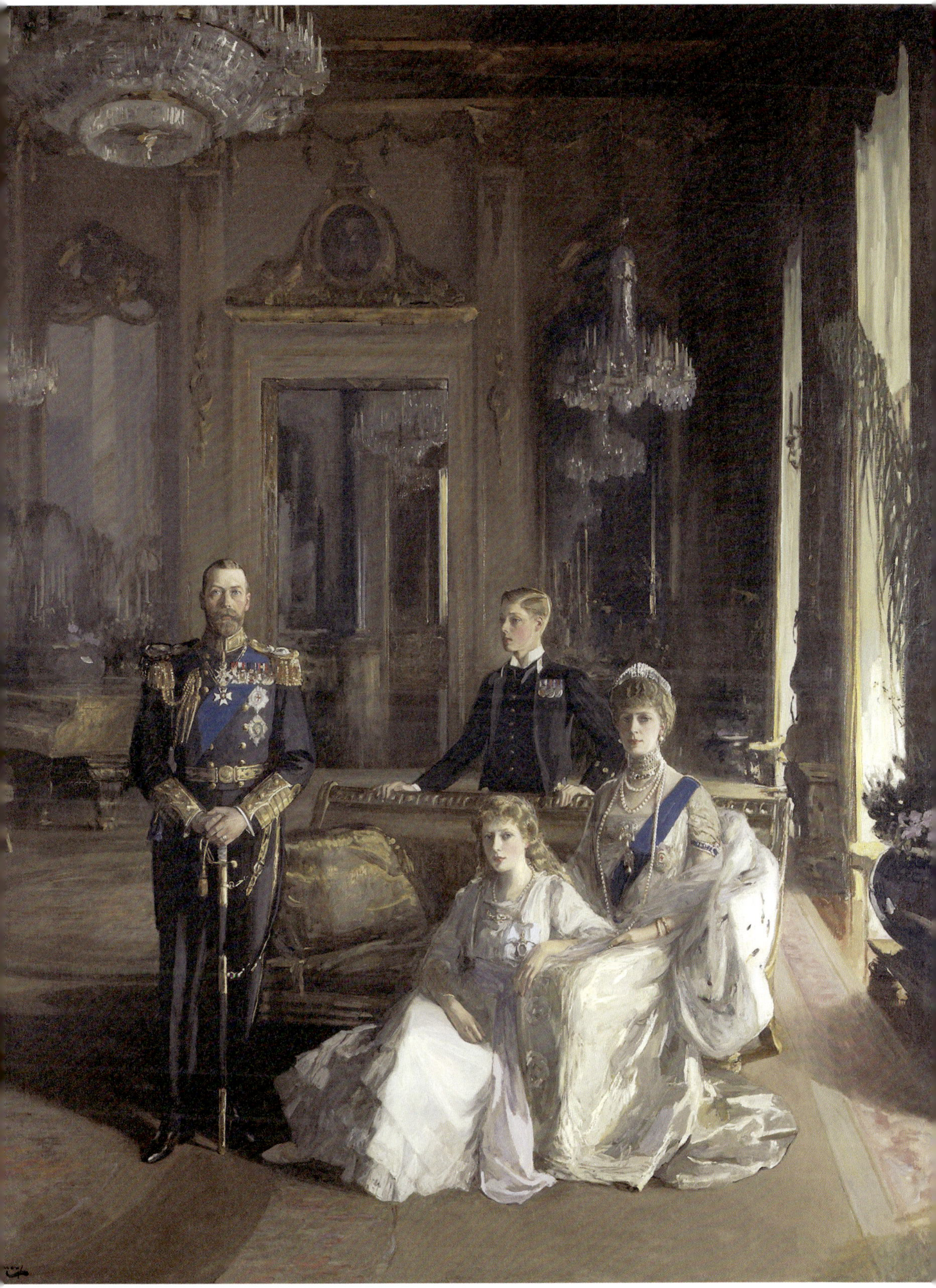

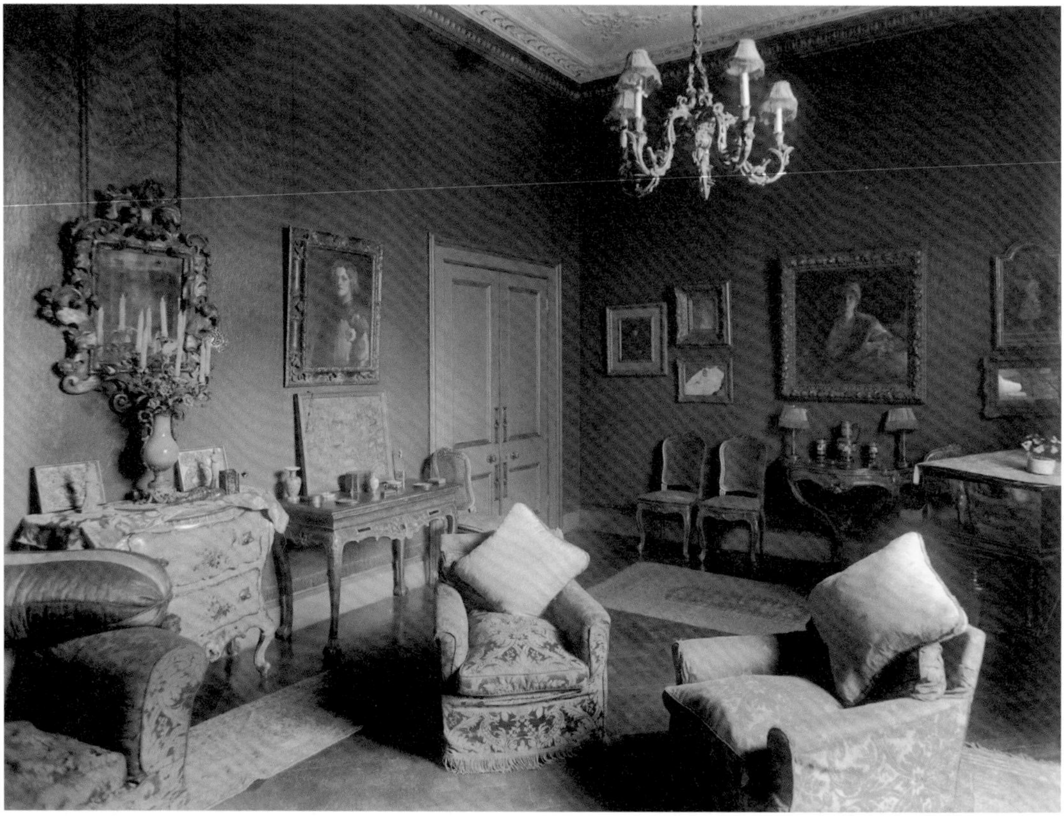

Bassano: *Sir John and Lady Lavery's Home (The Drawing Room)*, 28 October 1919
Glass plate negative
National Portrait Gallery, London

unsuccessful in getting her sister to stay in England. Lavery had recognised Hazel's difficulties and had urged her to give her sister into the care of a brain specialist, writing that August 1909: 'I expect as time goes on she deteriorates and her lucid intervals become briefer'.[71] Hazel had returned to Chicago to find that, tragically, her sister had died while she was making the transatlantic voyage. As Dorothy was being buried the newspapers ran stories speculating about what circumstances had led to the fact that a daughter of a once prominent family would die alone in a public hospital. The *Chicago Press* had run a headline, 'Deserted by sister'.[72] The news of her sister's tragic death did not, however, appear to have reached London society.[73]

Hazel was recorded in the press as a close friend of Margot Asquith, wife of the Prime Minister, whose circle was the wittiest in London. The Laverys spent time at the Asquiths' home, The Wharf at Sutton Courtenay, although Hazel preferred the company of Herbert Asquith to that of his wife. Society columns enthused that Hazel was a brilliant talker, suggesting that 'any woman who wanted to make her dinner party a go invites Hazel Lavery to be her guest'.[74] In private the women were not so kind. Cynthia Asquith, daughter-in-law of the Prime Minister, wrote in her diary: 'Hazel Lavery is a bore at a small party ... she never listens and entirely checks my flow'.[75] The social round was good for business, and so was the publicity, as Hazel's name, image and pictures of her home were featured in *The Tatler*, *The Lady's Pictorial* and *The Illustrated London News*: 'Mr John Lavery brought his pretty wife in black with a blue Russian toque and large necklace to match.'[76] On another occasion the reporter noted: 'The best dressed women in town are wearing no jewellery, save, perhaps, a necklace of pearls. Mrs Lavery, I noticed yesterday, no jewellery, only a flower tucked into her simple frock'.[77]

When the fashion house of Reville and Rossiter, who numbered Queen Mary among their clients, offered to dress her, Hazel refused, preferring instead to wear clothes of her own creation.[78] This was an economic decision as, no longer able to

71 Hazel Lavery to John Lavery, August 1909, quoted in McCoole, *Hazel*, p. 38.

72 Her sister Dorothy died on 13 October 1911. The cause of death was described on her death certificate as acute enteritis. Acute mania was cited as a contributing factor.

73 Even in her private papers Hazel would change dates on family photographs; it can be argued that the intention was to conceal the facts of her sister's death.

74 Unidentified press cutting, Lady Lavery Scrapbooks (private collection).

75 The Diaries of Lady Cynthia Asquith 1915–1918, London, 1987, p. 409. Entry: 4 February 1918, quoted in McCoole, *Hazel*, p. 52.

76 Unidentified press cutting, Lady Lavery Scrapbooks (private collection).

77 Unidentified press cutting, Lady Lavery Scrapbooks (private collection).

78 Morris manuscript (private collection).

afford high fashion, she sought the assistance of a Pimlico seamstress, Miss Hodges, to create her clothes. Cecil Beaton, while still at school, would cut Hazel's pictures out of magazines.[79] He would later remark that he had discovered that 'her clothes were generally concocted by herself and her maid. She would appear in public wearing organdie frills and a picture hat that she had pinned herself. The result was the best picturesque style … often she met with failure in these home made efforts. Once she became so irritated she burnt a fur muff'.[80] Hazel continued to assemble her own archive, recording her escalating profile in London society with the assistance of a news-clipping service.

Lavery was 'quite in vogue, and it was the time for every lady who was anybody in society, and could afford it, to have her portrait painted by Lavery'.[81] Meanwhile, he continued experimenting with Hazel's image. *Lady Lavery in Bed*, also known as *The Yellow Bed*[82] (untraced), caused considerable controversy with journalists when it was shown at the Portrait Painters exhibition. One cartoonist suggested that John Lavery would now be portraying people at their toilet or in the bath with the caption: 'at next year's Royal Academy perhaps Sir John Lavery's picture of his wife in bed may have started a new style in portraiture'.[83] Hazel said he used her as his sitter because it was cheaper. She joked that he would say 'Off with her head and on with yours' if it suited his mood.[84] One journalist wrote: 'Circumstances, too, have dealt unkindly with the Provosts, Professors, and Politicians in giving Mr. Lavery a wife who offers a perpetual invitation to portraiture that is not masculine'.[85] For Lavery, painting Hazel was often simply a break from commissioned work or just for the pleasure of depicting her in a new setting, as the canvases produced during their holiday in Wengen in Switzerland in November 1912 show: *A Winter Afternoon*, 1912; *Japanese Winter*, 1912, (Auckland Art Gallery McKelvie Trust Collection) and *Japanese Switzerland*, 1913 (Dublin City Gallery The Hugh Lane, on loan from a private collection). Lavery recorded: 'On our last day at Wengen I had to finish my

79 Alice McEnery Gwynn to Sinéad McCoole, Interview 26 March 1991.

80 Cecil Beaton, *The Wandering Years 1922–1939*, London, 1961, p. 271.

81 *Irish Times* Obituary for John Lavery, January 1941, Scrapbook belonging to Alice McEnery (private collection).

82 Sinéad McCoole, *The Yellow Bed*, RTE Radio 1, *Sunday Miscellany*, broadcast 9 May 2004.

83 Unidentified press cutting, Lady Lavery Scrapbooks (private collection).

84 Hazel Lavery to Arthur Deane (8 May 1929), quoted in McCoole, *Hazel*, p. 55.

85 Unidentified press cutting Lady Lavery Scrapbooks (private collection).

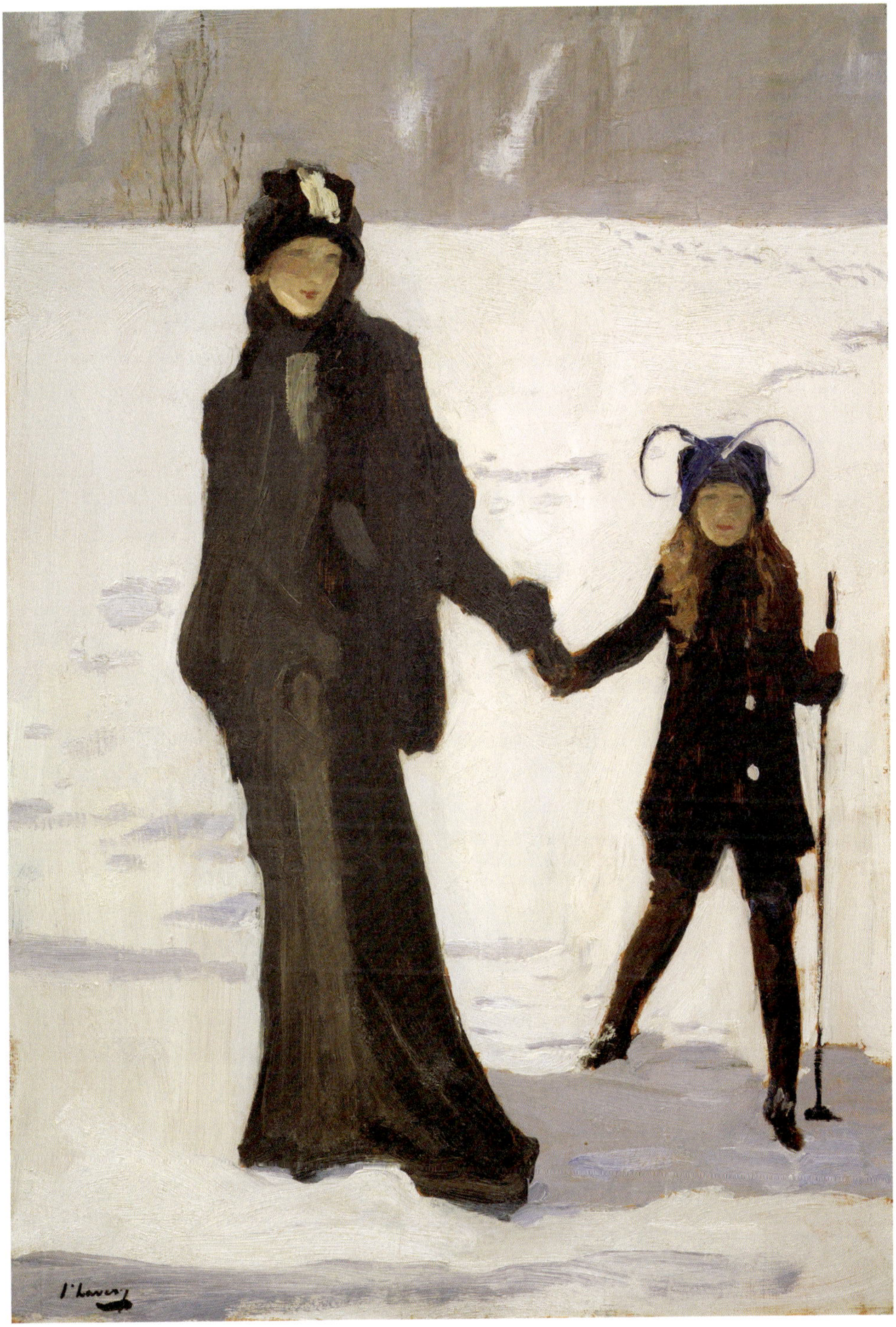

Japanese Switzerland, 1913
Oil on board, 76.1 × 53.3 cm
Dublin City Gallery The Hugh Lane Loan Collection

"Japanese Switzerland" – Hazel and Alice in the snow – and they were very patient; but as time went on and Alice saw how little of it would be left for a run on her luge, I heard her say to her mother, "Isn't it a pity, Muffie, that we married an artist?"'[86]

In 1913 Hazel was named as a new contributor to the International Show at the Grosvenor Gallery, where she exhibited a charcoal and coloured chalk portrait of the Russian dancer Anna Pavlova (Museum of London) whom Lavery had been commissioned to paint.[87] Described as the 'talented and beautiful wife of Mr. John Lavery A.R.A.', the work was 'meritorious'.[88] Hazel was also still making etchings which, it was reported, were in considerable demand by collectors.[89] Hazel knew that 'Hazell' the artist, as she sometimes styled herself, was not as valuable as Hazel the subject. Her role as muse became more important. She came to real prominence at the Fancy Dress Balls that were then in fashion among the social elite of London in the first decade of the 20th century. It was reported that 'Mrs Lavery is devoted to art and has been at most of the recent costume balls in magnificent dresses which display very clearly her own original and artistic taste'.[90] Hazel would take her inspiration from paintings: in December 1913 she was persuaded to go to the London Picture Ball as Sandro Botticelli's Flora from *Primavera*, c.1482 (Uffizi Gallery, Florence) – 'The boldest thing she was ever persuaded to do was to impersonate Botticelli's figure of Spring, and even that – the impossible – was a success'.[91] Her costume was worked with the finest details and wire was placed in the fine fabric to make it appear as if it was blowing in a breeze. This image was reproduced in magazines as far away as Germany.[92]

Hazel was now a sought-after model; one of those who photographed her was Baron de Meyer. The Frenchman is known to many as the founder of fashion photography but it was Hazel's collaboration with another photographer, the German Emil Otto Hoppé, who really created her public image. In 1913 he moved into 7 Cromwell Place, the former home of the artist John Everett Millais, and later

86 Lavery, *Life*, p. 208.
87 Unidentified press cutting, Lady Lavery Scrapbooks (private collection).
88 Unidentified press cutting, Lady Lavery Scrapbooks (private collection).
89 Unidentified press cutting, Lady Lavery Scrapbooks (private collection).
90 Unidentified press cutting, Lady Lavery Scrapbooks (private collection).
91 Unidentified press cutting, Lady Lavery Scrapbooks (private collection).
92 Unidentified press cutting, Lavery File (Witt Library, Courtauld Institute, London).

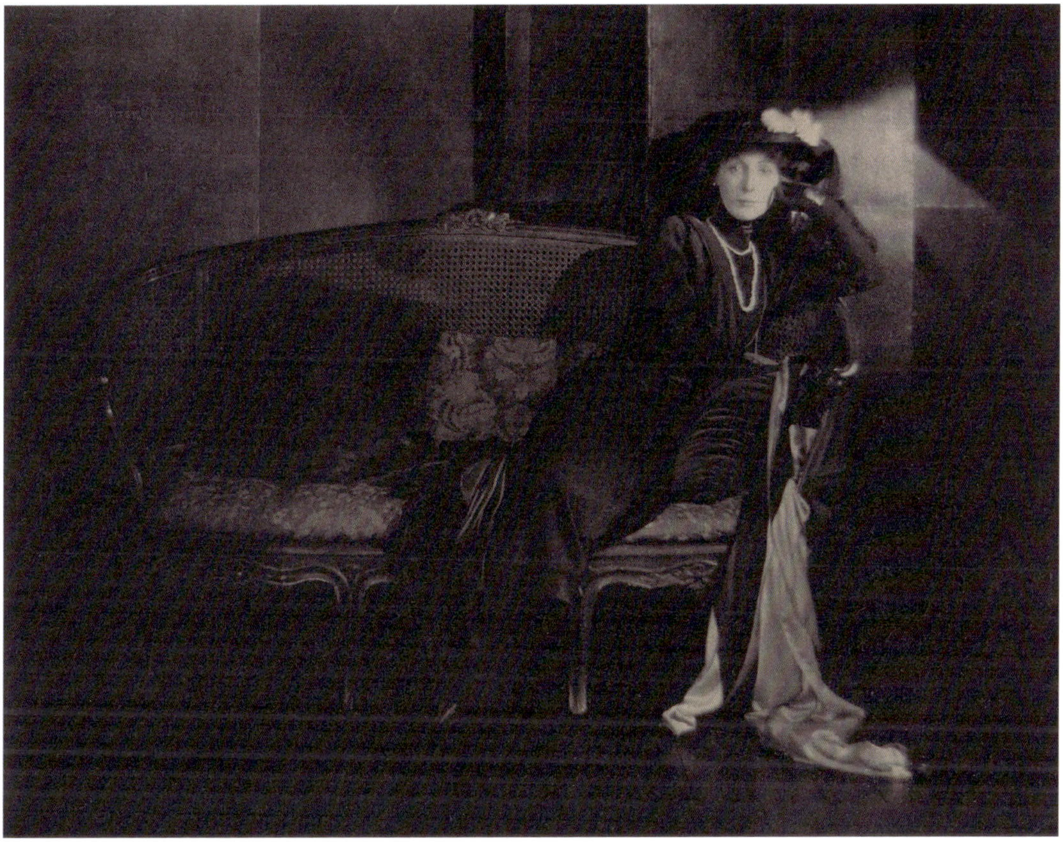

Baron Adolf de Meyer:
Hazel (née Martin), Lady Lavery, 1910
Vintage bromide print, 17.1 × 22.2 cm
National Portrait Gallery, London

that of Francis Bacon. Hazel was often seen running across the road in a variety of costumes to pose for him. It was a mutually beneficial arrangement; from that point forward Hoppé supplied images of Hazel to the press, full-page spreads of his photographs. Hoppé would later state that Hazel was one of the most beautiful women he had ever photographed.[93] In 1914 one of a series of Hoppé's images was of Hazel in furs and a richly patterned wrap, posing with her young Moroccan servant,[94] who was then about eight years old. Lavery knew the value of these images, as he knew the value of his own paintings of her. While McConkey comments on Lavery depicting Hazel in 'a selection of different guises', it was Hoppé's images of Hazel that were an important part of building the cult status of the Laverys and ensuring their continuing success.

In June 1914, at the American Peace Ball at the Albert Hall, London, Hazel posed as her home State, 'Illinois', in a pageant. She was in the company of other American ladies married to prominent or titled Englishmen, including Lady Harcourt, Lady Beatty, Lady Craven and the Hon. Mrs Freddy Guest. Interestingly, she was not featured in the press coverage of the event.[95] Her fame would really come as a result of the *tableaux vivants*[96] that became a popular method of fundraising by society ladies from the start of the First World War in 1914. Again it was Hoppé who made photographic records of these temporary 'living pictures', which were usually based on well-known paintings. Hazel stage-managed her image. She really enjoyed the preparation, as she remarked: 'The greatest fun of all is the making up, which takes at least six hours.'[97] She could take direction, for as the accomplished artist's model she had perfected posing for her husband and others. She 'knew all the tricks' and took control of the setting, instructing the electrician at one event to take out the amber lights, saying: 'they are hideously unbecoming – nothing like plain white chorus-girl lighting!'[98]

One of the first *tableaux vivants* Hazel took part in was for the British Women's Hospital, when she appeared as an Angel in a *tableau* after a painting by Rembrandt.[99]

93 Terence Pepper, *Camera Portraits by E.O. Hoppé (1878–1972)*, exhibition catalogue, National Portrait Gallery, London, 1978, p. 6.

94 He was the son of their Moroccan cook, Ben Ali. The boy stayed with the Laverys for only two years, as he hated the British climate and was bitterly unhappy in London.

95 *The Sphere*, 20 June 1914; *The Graphic*, 20 June 1914.

96 *Tableaux vivants* or living pictures were posed by artists' models or actors and actresses. Those who posed were silent and unmoving.

97 Josephine Ross, *Beaton in Vogue*, London, 1986, p. 31.

98 Ibid.

99 Unidentified press cutting, Lady Lavery Scrapbooks (private collection).

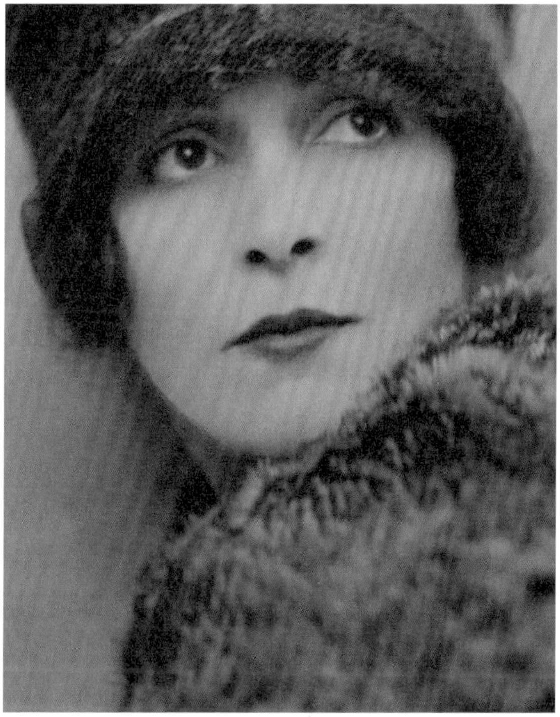

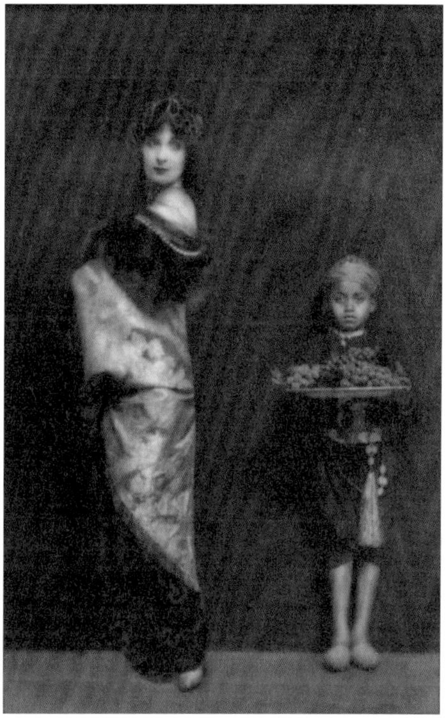

E.O. Hoppé: *Lady Lavery*, 1916

E.O. Hoppé Estate / Curatorial Assistance

E.O. Hoppé: *Lady Lavery and Boy*, 1914

E.O. Hoppé Estate / Curatorial Assistance

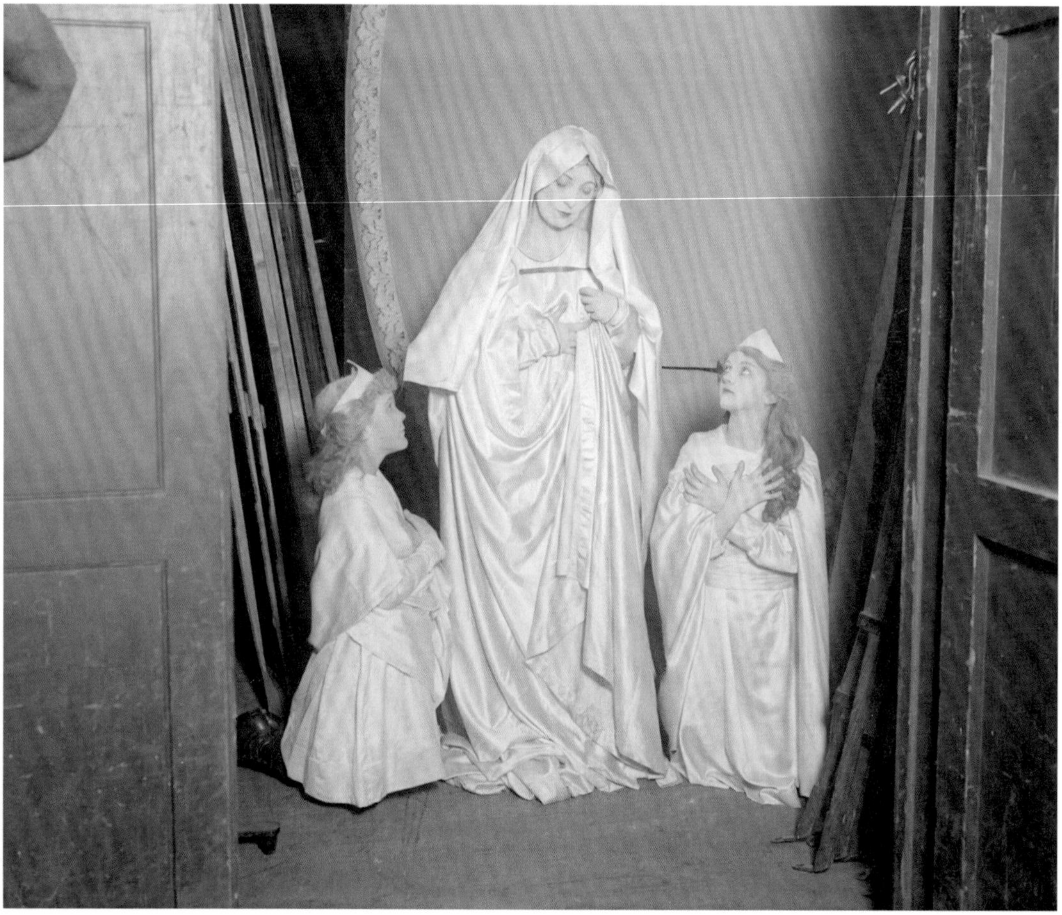

Misses Kinloc and Lowther with Lady Lavery in a *tableau* entitled 'A Lucca Della Robbia' at a matinee in aid of the Blue Cross, organised by Lady Lowther, 2nd May 1918

J. J. Lambe / Topical Press Agency / Getty Images

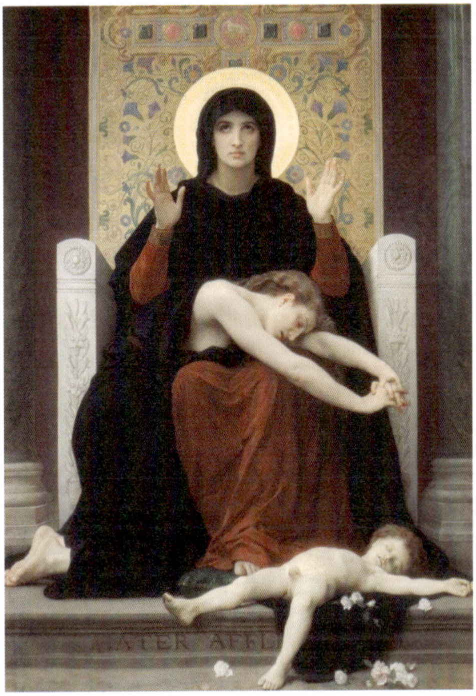

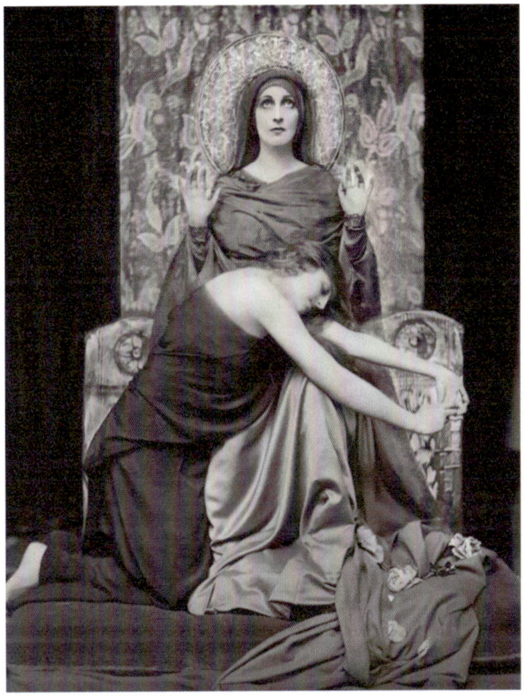

William Adolphe Bouguereau: *Vierge Consolatrice*, 1877
Oil on canvas, 204 × 148 cm
Musée des Beaux-Arts de Strasbourg

E.O. Hoppé: *Lady Lavery in 'La Vierge Consolatrice'*, 1916
E.O. Hoppé Estate / Curatorial Assistance

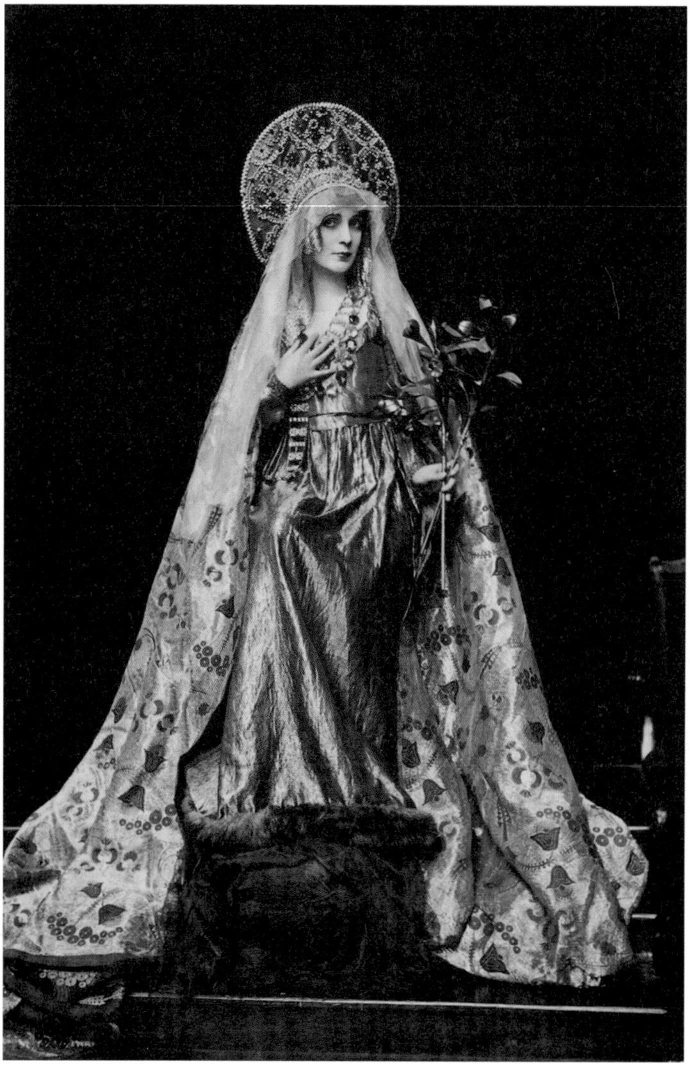

E.O. Hoppé: *Lady Lavery in 'The Miracle'*, 1916

E.O. Hoppé Estate / Curatorial Assistance

In June 1916 Hazel took part in a *tableau* based on a work by her husband's former teacher, the French artist William A. Bouguereau, *La Vierge Consolatrice*, 1877 (Musée de Strasbourg). This was one of seven *tableaux* produced in the home of a Mrs Leeds to raise funds for the Women's United Services League. According to reports 'La Vierge Consolatrice' depicted the Virgin Mary seated, in a blue mantle, while across her knees was a broken-hearted girl seeking consolation. Violet de Trafford posed as the 'fallen woman', a role turned down by Lady Nancy Cunard and Lady Diana Manners. Hazel was described as 'the rapt, ideal face of Mrs. Lavery, surrounded by a halo of dull gold, her virgin blue mantle falling in close folds, her hands outstretched'.[100] It was said that the success of her Bouguereau Madonna was so marked that she would be cast as the Madonna for life.[101] Hazel did appear again as the Madonna in an Italian matinée at the Savoy Theatre in aid of the Italian Red Cross,[102] where, in a pink and gold robe, she was the central figure of the Madonna in a *tableau* of a fifteenth-century triptych. She was flanked by Hon. Miss Lawley as St Michael and Miss Boyd as St Katherine. Lavery had arranged this *tableau* in a gold shrine and it was hailed it as the 'artistic triumph of the series'.[103]

Working on this *tableau* gave Lavery the idea of depicting his wife as the Madonna. He began work on a triptych he called *The Madonna of the Lakes*, again using family members as models. Alice posed as St Patrick as a boy, which critics correctly commented 'looked like a girl masquerading'.[104] Eileen was the model for St Brigid. 'Being influenced by the Italian conception of the Blessed Virgin, I painted her in gleaming robes of gold with nimbus, as I thought she might appear in a vision to simple-minded people, or, as I thought she might do to St Patrick, who is painted as a child and St Brigid who is portrayed as a shepherdess'.[105]

Lavery donated it to St Patrick's Roman Catholic Church, Donegall Street, the Belfast church in which he had been baptised. He proposed to build an extension to the church to house this work if required but this proved impossible so it was

100 Unidentified press cutting, Lady Lavery Scrapbooks (private collection).

101 Unidentified press cutting, Lady Lavery Scrapbooks (private collection).

102 Hazel was on the organising committee for this matinée along with Elizabeth Asquith, daughter of the Prime Minister. The meetings took place at 10 Downing Street.

103 'The Italian Matinée', unidentified press cutting, Lady Lavery Scrapbooks (private collection).

104 *The Manchester Guardian*, 7 May 1917, quoted in McConkey, 2010, p.232.

105 *The Irish News*, 21 April 1932, quoted in Ian Chant-Sempill, unpublished manuscript on Sempill Family.

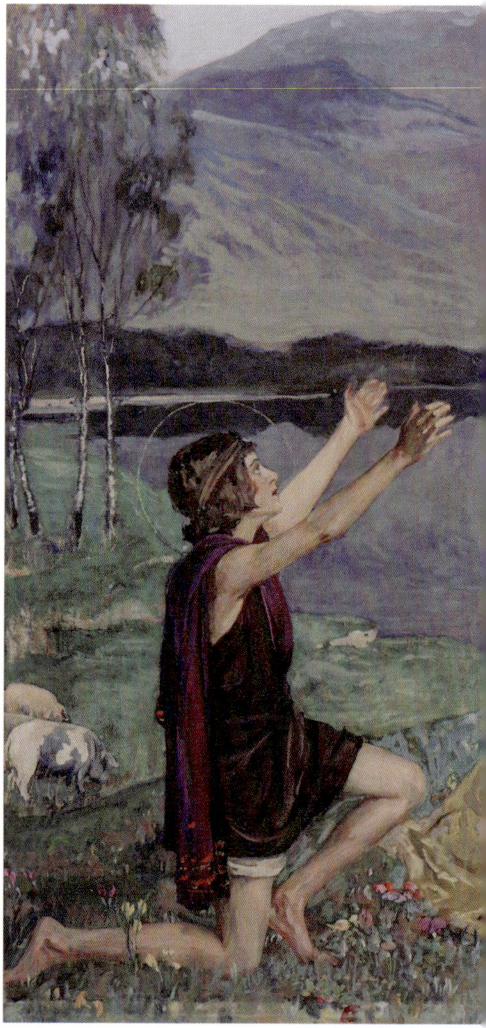

The Madonna of the Lakes, 1917
Oil on canvas, triptych, 277 × 385 cm (framed)
The Parish of St Patrick, Belfast

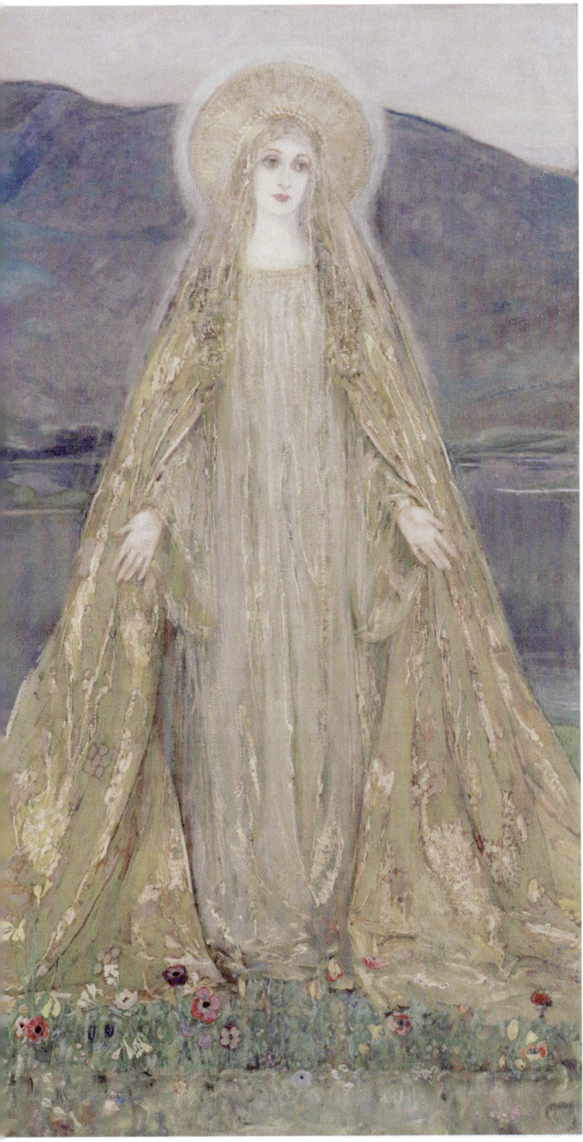

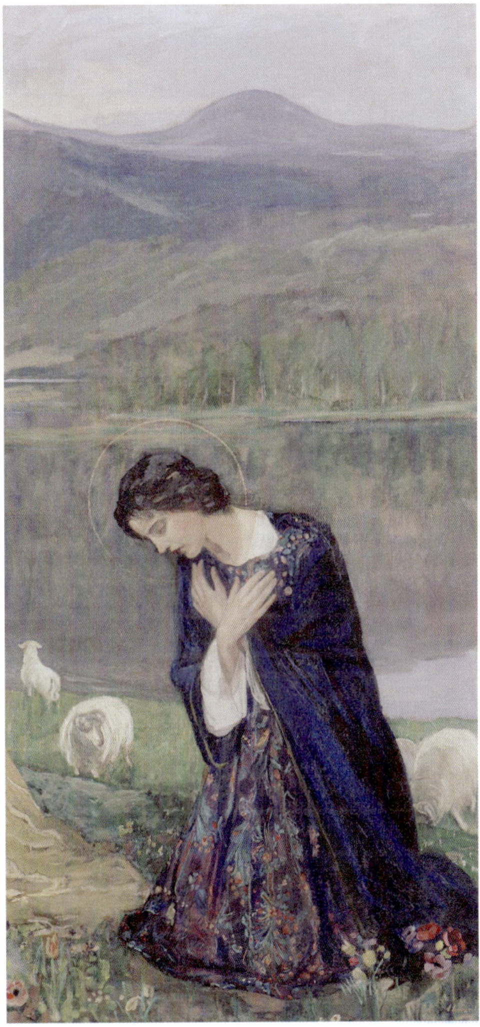

No. 863, January 9, 1918] *THE TATLER*

"OUR LADY OF PITY"

The Wife of a Famous Artist as She Appeared at a Recent Charity Matinée in a Tableau Designed by Mr. Glyn Philpot.

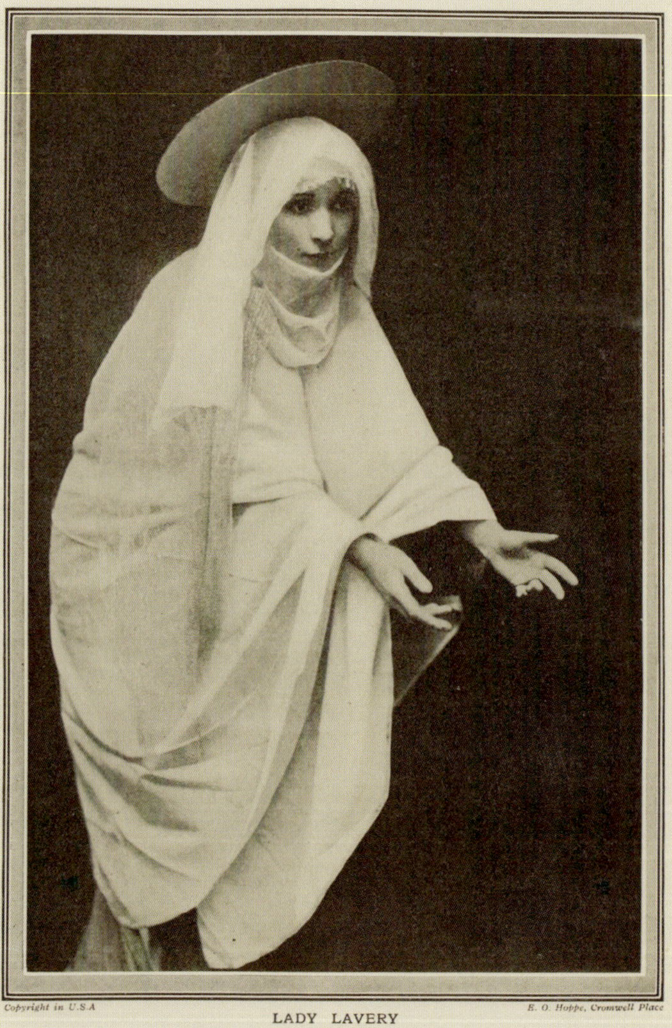

Copyright in U.S.A *E. O. Hoppe, Cromwell Place*

LADY LAVERY

Lady Lavery is the wife of one of the New Year knights, Sir John Lavery, the famous artist whose canvases enjoy a world-wide reputation. Lady Lavery is here seen posed as "Our Lady of Pity," after the design of Mr. Glyn Philpot, A.R.A., at the matinée which took place at the Vaudeville Theatre on January 4, and which was in aid of the funds of the Sisters of Mercy and their homes for working women and girls. The matinée was under the patronage of his Eminence the Cardinal Archbishop of Westminster, and the programme included a variety of items in which society and the stage were about equally represented

43

Lady Lavery as 'Our Lady of Pity', *The Tatler*, 9 January 1918. Photograph by E.O. Hoppé

Courtesy of the National Library of Ireland

necessary to accommodate the large artwork in the body of the church. He commissioned his friend Sir Edwin Lutyens[106] to design a frame for the work. The frame with its old Gaelic script and Celtic motifs was similar to work being produced in Ireland at the time in places like the Cuala Industries. At this time Lavery wrote that he wanted to 'help the artistic life of the city' and had formed the idea of presenting works to Belfast Corporation.[107]

Hazel's appearance as Madonna had not caused offence and she again appeared in this role in order to raise funds for the Catholic Church. The *tableaux vivants* continued, and in January 1918 she was styled by the artist Glyn Philpot as 'Our Lady of Pity' at the Vaudeville Theatre, London, in aid of the Sisters of Mercy and their homes for working women and girls, a programme under the patronage of the Cardinal Archbishop of Westminster.[108]

It was a natural evolution in her artistic progress that Hazel should develop from artist's model through *tableaux vivants* to become an actress in plays and on film. She was a member of Hoppé's private theatre group known as 'the Plough Theatre Club', which was formed to produce plays that had not been staged in Britain. Between 1917 and 1919 they produced several plays, including Clifford Bax's *The Sneezing Charm*. In 1918 Hazel took part in D.W. Griffith's film *Hearts of the World*, a silent movie starring Lillian Gish, which was filmed in France. She was one of a number of society ladies who were cast in minor roles; she is credited on the film in the role of a nurse.[109] One newspaper reported that 'the smart craze at the moment is to be filmed for a picturesque part in the tremendous new war play'.[110]

106 Sir Edwin Lutyens is sometimes described as the arts and craft architect. He had been knighted for his work in New Delhi, India. In 1917 he was one of the principal architects of the Imperial War Graves commission, and was responsible for the Irish National War Memorial, Islandbridge, Dublin. He did designs for Hugh Lane for his proposed gallery in Dublin, including one gallery that would span the river Liffey, but these were never completed. He designed Hazel's gravestone.

107 John Lavery papers (The Parish of St Patrick, Belfast).

108 Unidentified press cutting, Lady Lavery Scrapbooks (private collection).

109 I am grateful to Logan Sisley for sourcing this reference.

110 Unidentified press cutting, Lady Lavery's Scrapbooks (private collection).

The Laverys were in Ireland when war was declared in 1914. Hazel returned home to find a letter from her friend Duff Cooper[111] sent on 5 August 1914 from the Foreign Office in Whitehall in which he told her: 'I with my own hands sent off the ultimatum to Germany. I will tell you all about it when you come back.'[112]

The Laverys' first recorded visit to Ireland was in 1913, when they stayed by the Killarney lakes with Lord and Lady Kenmare at Killarney House. Ever the chameleon, from this time onwards Hazel was keen to say that she was 'a simple Irish girl', a Martyn from Galway. When she met the writer Edward Martyn[113] she tried to convince him that she was a relative but he disagreed, telling her he had no beauties in his family.[114] Lavery was well aware of this deliberate fabrication. In his autobiography, written after Hazel's death, he would describe her version of Ireland as 'as unreal as a mirage in a desert'.[115] Lavery read the Irish newspapers and was known to have read passages from the *Freeman's Journal* to Prime Minister Asquith when they were together, an indication that he was keeping in touch with events in Ireland. Lavery stated in his autobiography that it was Hazel who had suggested that he use his art to reconcile the opposing sides.[116]

Irish politics was in a period of change. In 1914, the Home Rule Bill awaiting ratification in the British parliament was put on hold when war was declared. In Ulster, Edward Carson[117] rallied those wishing to remain under British rule (the Unionists). The Ulster Volunteer Force was formed to resist Home Rule by force if necessary. In the south, the nationalist leader, John Redmond, leader of the Irish Parliamentary Party, was at the height of his power with the promised Home Rule Bill.[118] In 1916 Lavery arranged sittings with Carson and Redmond, agreeing with them in advance that their portraits would hang side by side in a Dublin gallery.[119] When Redmond heard of Lavery's plan he replied: 'I have always had an idea that Carson and I might someday be hanged side-by-side in Dublin.'[120] When the portraits were completed, Carson thought that Redmond's portrait was better and,

111 Duff Cooper, later Lord Norwich, married society beauty Lady Diana Manners. They had a son John Julius Norwich.

112 Duff Cooper to Hazel Lavery, quoted in McCoole, *Hazel*, p. 57.

113 Edward Martyn the dramatist, from Tulira Castle, County Galway, was a founder member of the Irish Literary Theatre, the Irish Theatre Company, the Palestrina Choir and the Feis Ceoil.

114 She always distanced herself from what she described as that 'awful thing, an Irish American'; see McCoole, *Hazel*, p. 63.

115 Lavery, *Life*, p. 221.

116 Lavery, *Life*, p. 208.

117 Edward Carson was the Solicitor General for both Ireland and England, and from 1910 the leader of the Unionists.

118 John Redmond was the leader of the Irish Parliamentary Party from 1900–1919. His dream of a united Ireland, which once seemed a possibility, diminished after 1912 and from 1916 his political power was in decline because of his support for the British War effort and the events of the 1916 Rising.

119 The paintings were donated by Lavery to the sale in aid of the Irish War Hospital Supply Depot and purchased and donated to the Municipal Gallery (now Dublin City Gallery The Hugh Lane) by Lieutenant-Colonel Hutcheson-Poë in 1917, in remembrance of Hugh Lane.

120 Ibid.

knowing that Lavery was a Belfast Catholic, remarked, 'It's easy to see which side you're on.'[121] The artist later said of his action: 'That was my first attempt to bind up the contending forces in the bonds of holy paint.'[122]

The whole Irish political landscape changed completely in 1916 when a small group of nationalists decided that while Britain was at war they would use the opportunity to rise in rebellion. The group, lead by the Provisional Government of the Irish Republic (the authorities mistakenly called them Sinn Féiners), planned a Rising to take place at Easter 1916. In planning for the Rising Sir Roger Casement,[123] a former British diplomat and humanitarian, attempted to land arms but the shipment was intercepted off the Kerry coast. The arms were being smuggled in from Germany. Casement was arrested. Despite the arrest of Casement and the capture of the arms, the Rising went ahead. After seven days of fighting, P.H. Pearse surrendered on behalf of the Provisional Government of the Irish Republic, thousands were rounded up and imprisoned and fifteen men[124] who had taken part in the Rising were executed by firing squad. Casement was taken to London and charged with treason. His trial was held in London in the summer of 1916.

Although there was an appeal, the result was a foregone conclusion. Chief Justice Darling later described it to John Lavery as 'one of Her Majesty's Government's victories over the benches.'[125] Lavery was permitted to sit in the court and painted the scene of Judge Charles Darling presiding over Casement's appeal to his sentence of death in July 1916. While he worked in the jury box, Lavery thought: 'In the drowsy monotony of the talk that went on for two days it was difficult to realise a man's life was at stake.'[126] One of the prosecutors, F.E. Smith,[127] was disturbed by the idea of Lavery painting this image of the Casement appeal.[128] Newspaper reports conveyed the general shock that Lavery had accepted to do such a thing: 'Girls in White, Girls on the sands in full sun or girls on horseback – such used to be Lavery's themes. But the penalty of fame has brought him other subjects including a Coronation and a trial.

121 Lavery, *Life*, p.208.

122 'Sir John Lavery – His Works a Record of Modern Life', *Sunday Times*, c.1930, Lady Lavery Scrapbooks (private collection).

123 Roger Casement was born in Dublin in 1864. He joined the British Colonial Service in Africa in 1892. He earned international recognition and was knighted in 1911 for his work in exposing atrocities against native workers in the Belgian Congo and later in Peru. He joined the Irish Volunteers in 1913.

124 In addition to those who had signed the Proclamation of Independence – P.H. Pearse, Tom Clarke, Thomas MacDonagh, Eamonn Ceannt, Joseph Plunkett, Sean MacDiarmada and James Connolly – the authorities also sentenced Con Colbert, Michael Mallin, Major John MacBride, Michael O'Hanrahan, Willie Pearse, Edward Daly, Sean Heuston and Thomas Kent (in Cork) to death by firing squad.

125 Charles Darling to John Lavery, 1 January 1918 (Tate Archive).

126 Lavery, *Life*, p.190.

127 'The late FE' (Smith) (later Lord Chancellor becoming Lord Birkenhead) thought of having the painting purchased as a historical document for the law courts. However, Lavery wrote: '... alas, I kept proposing its completion until it was too late as far as he was concerned.' John Lavery to J.H. Morgan, 14 December 1931 (Tate Archive, 7245.5).

128 F.E. Smith to John Lavery, quoted in Lavery, *Life*, p.189.

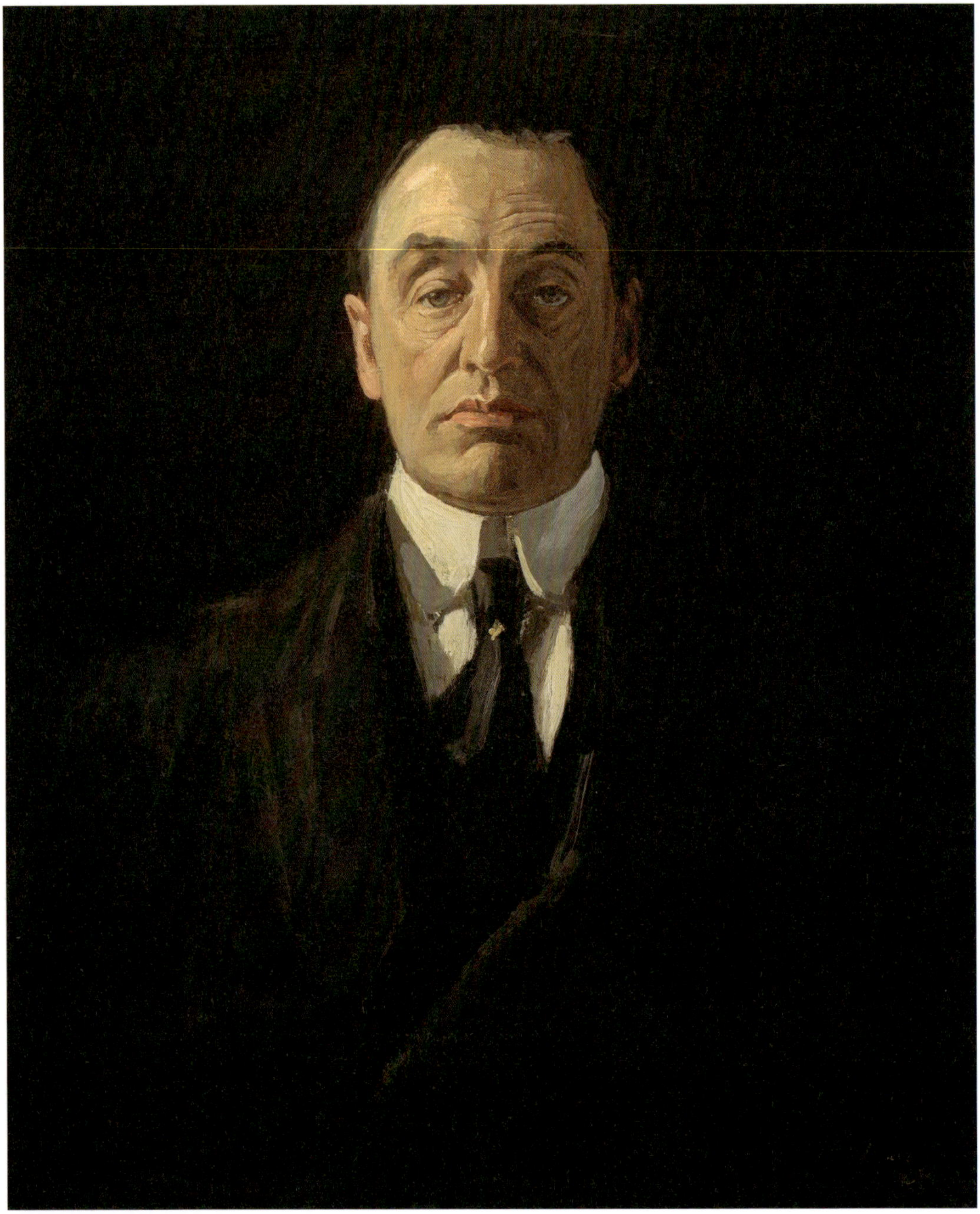

Sir Edward Carson, MP, 1916
Oil on canvas, 76.2 × 63.6 cm
Collection Dublin City Gallery The Hugh Lane

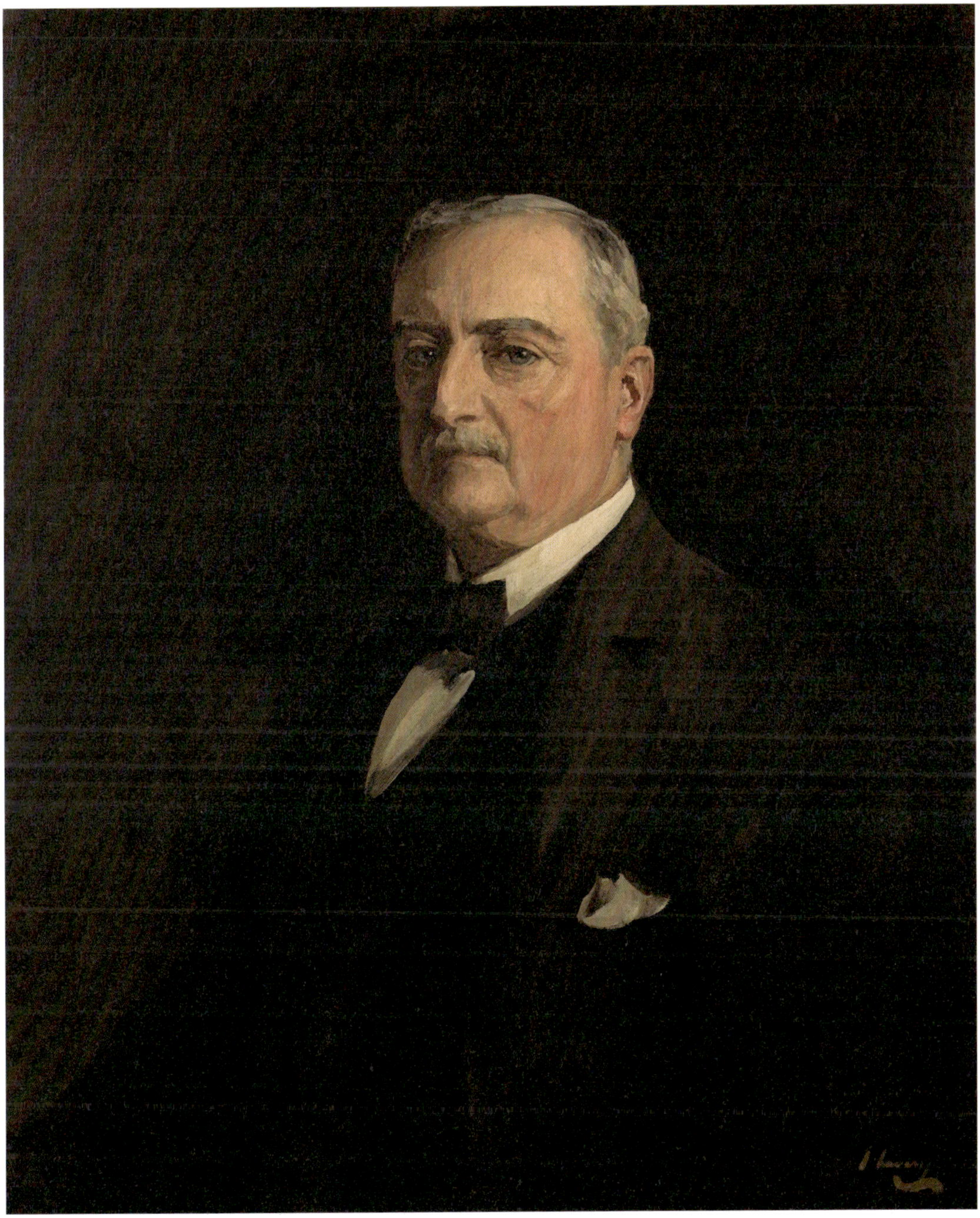

John E. Redmond, MP, 1916
Oil on canvas, 76.2 × 63.6 cm
Collection Dublin City Gallery The Hugh Lane

Of all the trials not to paint, the Casement trial I should have thought would have had first place. But Lavery, the debonair, had gone right through with the painful task ...'[129] The *Weekly Dispatch* reported: 'Much astonishment has been caused in artistic circles by the statement, so far uncontradicted, that Mr John Lavery is engaged in painting the final scene in the Casement trial ... Mr Lavery ought not to paint his picture without knowing the contents of the two diaries[130] ... from all of which it follows that the forthcoming picture is sure to attract immense attention but scarcely the kind of notice that so popular an artist is seeking.'[131]

Casement was hanged on 3 August 1916. Lavery continued to work on the painting of the Court of Criminal Appeal to ensure 'historical accuracy'. He set about gathering information and arranging sittings with those who had been present in court. As a result, he met those who had had an involvement with the Rising. He was looking for contact information for those present, including Eva Gore-Booth, sister of the so-called 'Rebel Countess', Constance Markievicz who at that time was serving life in prison for her part in the Rising. The wife of one of Casement's solicitors, Margaret Gavan Duffy, sent Lavery a letter detailing the information he requested: 'The lady in the gallery was Miss Eva Gore Booth the poet. She lives at 33 FitzRoy and is on the telephone. ... I enclose a photograph of Miss Ada McNeill ... who sat beside Mrs Parry nearest to Roger Casement. She is very dark with finely cut features – a beautiful woman. I think she wore purple ... But so long as Roger is lifelike what matter anyone else.'[132] In December, Lavery received a letter from Gertrude Parry, Sir Roger Casement's cousin, who supplied him with pictures. She also wrote how very important it was to her that the painter of her cousin's last days was an Irishman. She repeated what her cousin Roger had written to her from Pentonville Prison at the time of the Appeal: 'Who was the painter in the Jury box painting a picture of the court? I should think he came perilously near aiding and comforting, if indeed compassing, from the way he eyed Mr Justice Darling's delivery judgment ...'[133]

129 'Another Trial!', unidentified press cutting, Lady Lavery Scrapbooks (private collection).

130 The so-called Black Diaries exposed Casement's homosexuality and were widely circulated to counteract any sympathy that there might have been for the former diplomat.

131 *The Weekly Dispatch*, 22 October 1916 (Lavery Collection, Tate Archive 7245.8).

132 Margaret Gavan Duffy to John Lavery, 16 November 1916 (Tate Archive, 7245.1).

133 Gertrude Parry to John Lavery, quoted in Lavery, *Life*, pp. 189–190.

Lavery made a smaller version of the finished painting in oils, which is now in the collection of Dublin City Gallery The Hugh Lane. The finished work took a number of years to complete; Lavery was still working on it in the 1930s. There are differences between the preparatory sketch and the finished painting. The sketch includes the balcony where Hazel can be seen sitting, wearing a hat. In the finished work the gallery was omitted. The sketch is a more personalised version, as it contains more of the Irish supporters of Roger Casement.[134] Even before Lavery started work on this painting, he had given public support for the families of those who had been executed and imprisoned in the Rising by offering a portrait sitting[135] at a sale at the Mansion House in May 1916. Lavery's generosity to Irish Aid Funds was gratefully acknowledged by those who were active in the Irish independence movement.[136]

Lavery's support for the nationalist cause in Ireland ran alongside his unapologetic contact with loyalist Ireland. When visiting Ireland in September 1917, the Laverys stayed in the Viceregal Lodge in Phoenix Park as guests of the Lord Lieutenant. Hazel was impressed with the eighteenth-century house, and Lavery later wrote that, from that moment 'There was no other Ireland for her'.[137]

Meanwhile, throughout this period Lavery was working on behalf of the British Government as an official war artist. He had tried to enlist in the war as part of the regiment for artists, the Artists' Rifles, but his age was against him. He was accepted as a war artist to the Navy on the home front.[138] His assignments included complications such as taking to an airship to paint scenes in the North Sea, and dodging stones thrown by children who took him for a German spy.[139] One of Lavery's final assignments as a war artist was his painting of Admiral Sir David Beatty reading the terms of the Armistice to the German delegates in the fore-cabin of HMS *Queen Elizabeth* on 16 November 1918, a painting he entitled *The End* (Imperial War Museum, London).

134 In 1928 Lavery had 'turned it to the wall' and intended to complete it. In 1931 John H. Morgan, KC, enquired if it was completed and if it was for sale (Tate Archive, 7245.4). Lavery bequeathed the painting to the National Portrait Gallery, London, and if they did not want it then to the Royal Courts of Justice. It was accepted by the Lord Chancellor's Department for the Royal Courts. It is currently on loan to the King's Inns, Dublin.

135 *Irish Independent*, Easter Week 1966, reported that the canvas sold for £800. This work is untraced.

136 Margaret Gavan Duffy to John Lavery, 16 November 1916 (Tate Archive, 7245.1).

137 Lavery, *Life*, p. 221.

138 The paintings done by Lavery as war artist are now in the collection of the Imperial War Museum, London.

139 McConkey, 2010, p. 137.

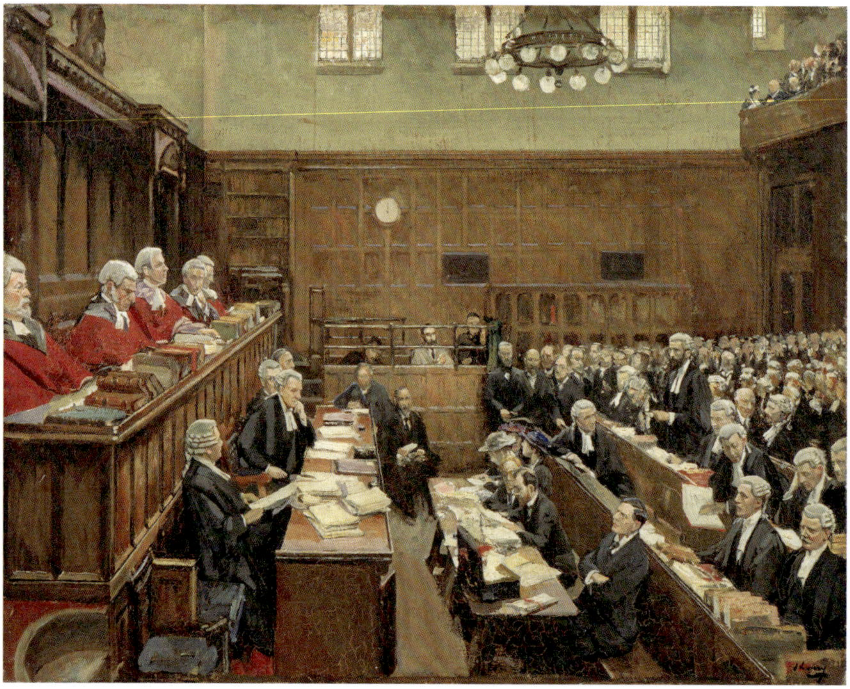

The Court of Criminal Appeal. The Trial of Sir Roger Casement, London, 1916, 1916
Oil on panel, 80 × 63.5 cm
Collection Dublin City Gallery The Hugh Lane

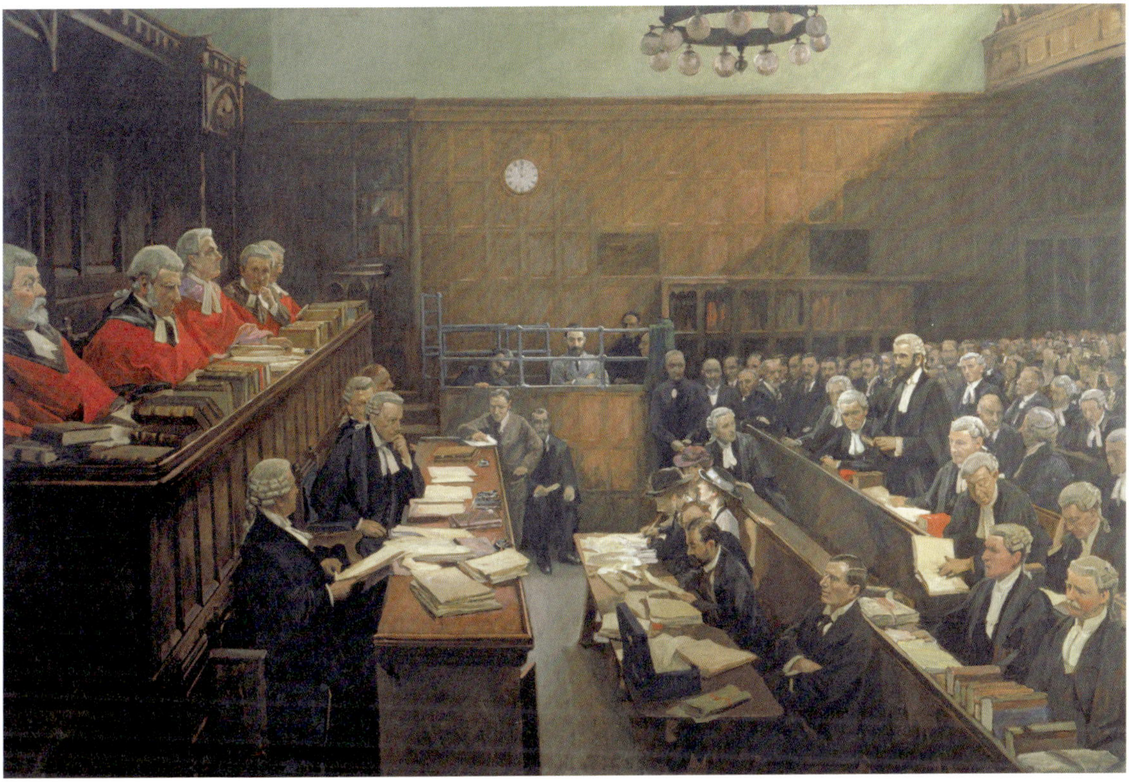

High Treason, Court of Criminal Appeal: the Trial of Sir Roger Casement, 1916
Oil on canvas, 194.5 × 302.5 cm
UK Government Art Collection

On Christmas Eve 1917 the British Prime Minister, David Lloyd George, had sent Lavery a letter to inform him that 'His Majesty has been pleased to approve of my recommendation that you should receive the honour of a Knighthood'.[140] In January 1918 he became Sir John Lavery,[141] which meant that the courtesy title of Lady Lavery[142] was bestowed on his wife.

Lavery used his affable personality to effect change and he set about painting portraits of prominent figures in Irish politics, aided by an elaborate network of friends. He continued his Irish collection of portraits, working on images of Protestant and Catholic religious leaders and politicians in Ireland. On a visit to Belfast while the First World War was continuing, Lavery lunched with the Unionist Lord Mayor of that city, and also attended a function with members of the Orange Order.'[143]

As the First World War came to an end, the Laverys once more travelled to Ireland, where, however, the Irish War of Independence was still ongoing. Following the 1918 election, the new political party, Sinn Féin, had established an underground Dáil Éireann with its own cabinet and law courts. They also had their own appointments in existing local government. Organised in a systematic fashion, they sought to undermine British rule in the country. A full-scale guerrilla war commenced, in 1919, with the first attack on the police force. In response to the campaign on the Royal Irish Constabulary and the Dublin Metropolitan the British Government drafted in new recruits in the RIC, and by October 1920 they numbered over 2,000. They were known as the Black and Tans on account of their uniforms. In July 1920 a separate force, the Auxiliaries, was drafted in, comprised mainly of former British military officers. The freedom fighters, now known as the Irish Republican Army, had formed what were called flying columns, which were based in villages, towns, cities and rural hideouts all over the country. The women formed *Cumann na mBan* (the council of women) and worked the secret organisation's communication system.

140 David Lloyd George to John Lavery, 24 December 1918, Lady Lavery Scrapbooks (private collection).

141 Lavery claimed in his autobiography that he had accepted the title for his wife's sake, but Hazel did not want to accept it because of British policy in Ireland during the War of Independence. However, those events did not take place until the following year. Lavery, *Life*, p. 212.

142 She joked that it sounded like ladies' lavatory and she was proved right when she said her name at an official function and was misheard and given directions. McCoole, *Hazel*. p. 62.

143 The Orange Order was founded in 1795 to preserve the Protestant religion and maintain the British monarchy and constitution. Since 1921 it has sought to protect and promote the position of the province of Northern Ireland within the United Kingdom.

In 1920 Lavery travelled to Armagh, the seat of the Roman Catholic Primate of Ireland, where Cardinal Michael Logue sat for him at the Archbishop's Palace. Hazel, who was with him, also did a pencil sketch of the Cardinal, who with his distinctive features was an ideal subject for portraiture.

The Laverys' close friend, Winston Churchill,[144] asked them for an assessment of the Irish situation. The letter of reply, written from Ireland, has much of Hazel's wording and she signed it first:

> 'You asked me the other day what I thought of my country's state, and I had not the courage to tell you. But if one artist can speak to another I will give you my beliefs. ... I believe that Ireland will never be governed by Westminster, the Vatican or Ulster without continuous bloodshed. I also believe the removal of the Castle and all its works, leaving Irishmen to settle their own affairs, is the only solution left. I am convinced with the knowledge I possess of my countrymen that such a situation would make her one of our staunchest allies instead of an avowed enemy for all time. Love is stronger than hate.'[145]

The Laverys continued their tour of Ireland, visiting such places as Bundoran a seaside town in County Donegal, Westport and Ballina in County Mayo, Athlone in County Westmeath and Maynooth in County Kildare. While it seemed a most unusual selection of towns, Lavery suggested that Hazel was searching for the elusive Michael Collins, the revolutionary leader, who was leading the offensive of the freedom fighters. Collins had risen to prominence when he was imprisoned[146] in the aftermath of the Rising. He was the Minister for Finance in the underground government known as the Dáil, and head of the spy network. The Laverys were targets of both sides. Churchill had warned them about their planned motoring holiday while guerrilla warfare was operating in Ireland saying, 'Be careful, my dear John, all our men are not all good shots.'[147]

144 This was no passing acquaintance, as the Laverys were his unofficial art teachers. Churchill, who rarely gave credit to women, always acknowledged Hazel's efforts to encourage him to paint after his dismissal from the Admiralty for the disastrous Dardanelles campaign in 1915.

145 Lavery, *Life*, pp. 211–212.

146 The internment camps were known as the Universities of Revolution, see Sean O'Mahony, *Frongoch*, 1987.

147 Winston Churchill quoted in Lavery, *Life*, p. 213.

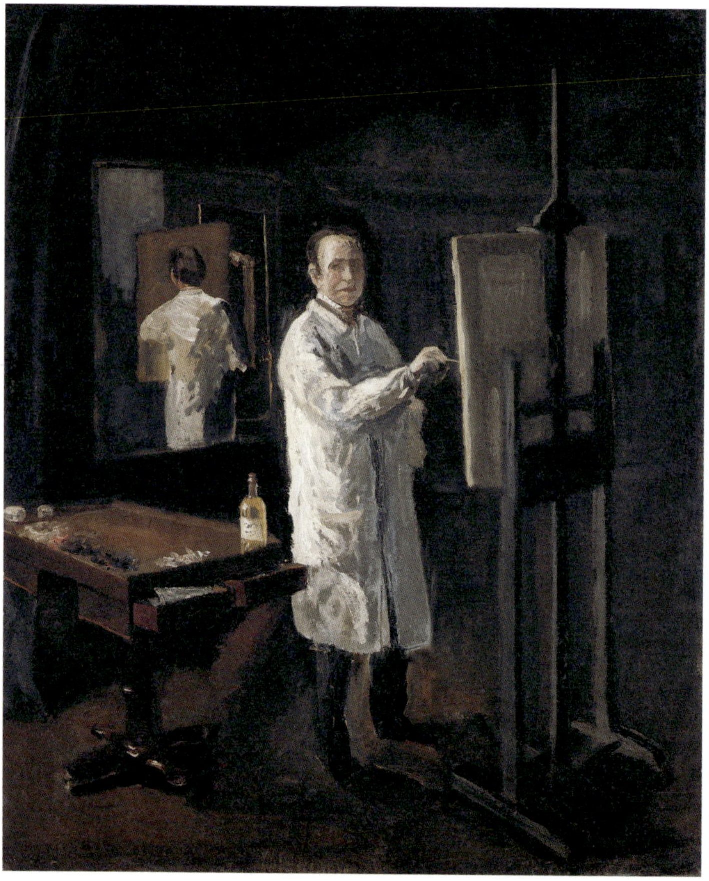

Winston Churchill: *Sir John Lavery in his Studio*, 1919
Oil on canvas, 76 × 63.5 cm
Private collection, on loan to National Trust, Chartwell

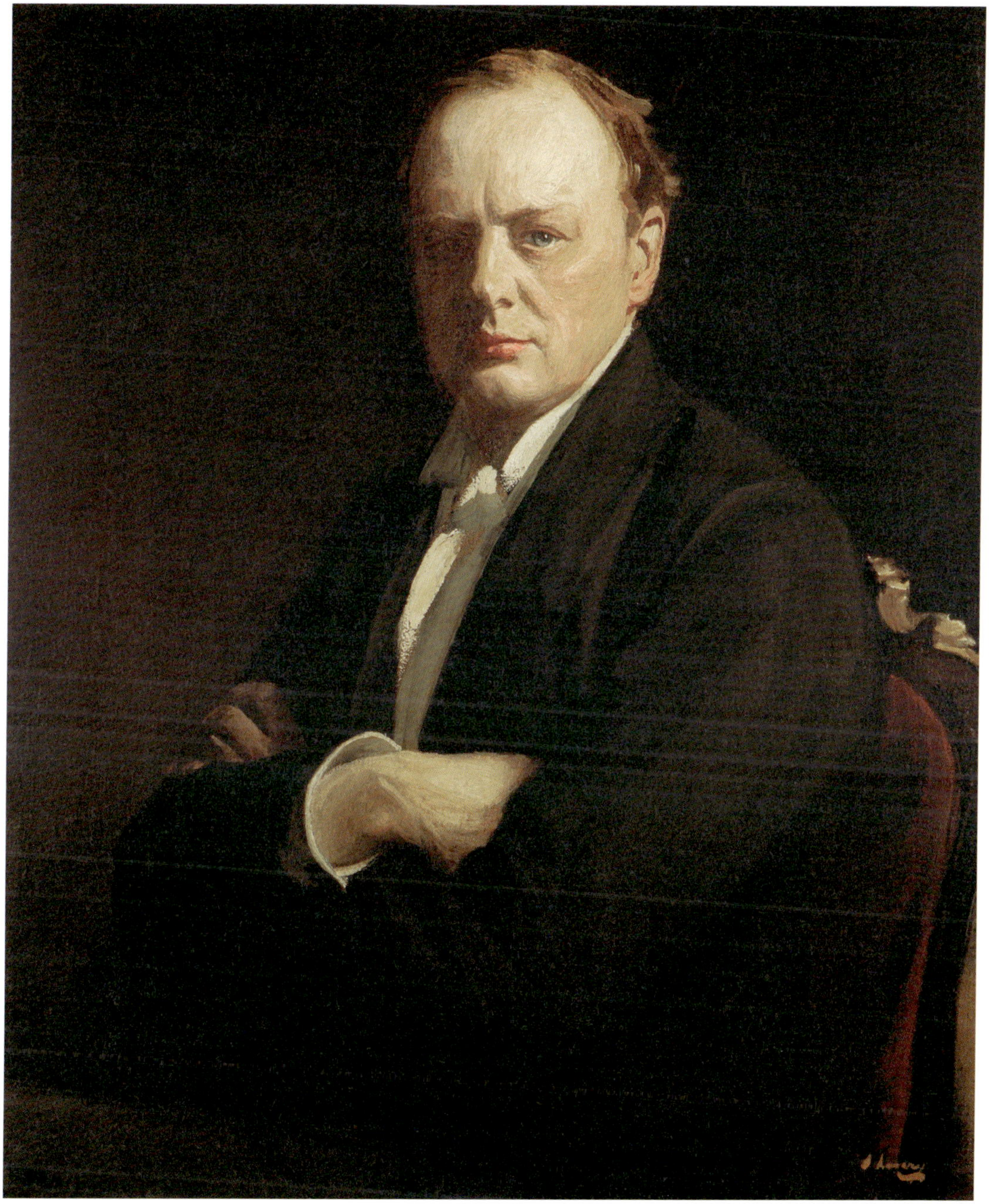

Sir Winston Churchill, 1915
Oil on canvas, 76.8 × 63.9 cm
Collection Dublin City Gallery The Hugh Lane

Lavery was now completely engrossed in Irish affairs. The vicious reign of the Black and Tans in Ireland had changed him; prior to their arrival he felt he had no patriotism or love of country. 'For years I did not grasp what Ireland had suffered, and if I did, the feeling was that it probably served us right. But when … the Black and Tans were given *carte blanche* to do their damnedest – which they did – the desire to fight stirred in my blood for the first time.'[148]

In October 1920 Lavery painted *Southwark Cathedral, London, 1920 (Terence MacSwiney)*. This painting shows Terence MacSwiney's coffin in Southwark Cathedral, before his remains were returned to Ireland. Forty-two year old Terence MacSwiney, Lord Mayor of Cork, who had died after seventy-four days on hunger-strike in Brixton Prison, which he had started in protest against the authority of the British court. Those, like MacSwiney, who had taken up public office for the political organisation Sinn Féin were more at risk of retaliation than those in the flying columns.[149] Lavery would later paint the portrait of MacSwiney's young widow, Muriel, a painting that is now in the Crawford Art Gallery in her native Cork.

By December 1920 the Government of Ireland Act had passed into law. It provided for two parliaments, one in Dublin and one in Belfast. The parliament for Northern Ireland came into existence in June 1921. At this stage the whole of Ireland remained in 'the United Kingdom of Great Britain and Ireland' with the British monarch as head of state. It was the King's[150] speech at the opening the Belfast Parliament that was the catalyst for the opening of negotiations with the proscribed parliament in Dublin, Dáil Éireann. A truce was agreed on 11 July 1921. In early July 1921 the Laverys cancelled their summer plans in order to make themselves available to the Irish delegates who were in London to negotiate a peace settlement with the British. Hazel, a noted hostess and interior designer,[151] wanted to invite the most elusive leader Michael Collins to her salon. In order to secure his attendance she contacted his sister Johanna, who worked in Kensington.[152]

148 Lavery, *Life*, p.207.

149 Two other Lord Mayors had been killed by the Black and Tans.

150 King George V's speech was a personal appeal by him at this formal occasion.

151 Interior design could have been Hazel's career as she was noted for her skill in making table arrangements for friends.

152 Johanna (Hanna) Collins when asked for her assessment of Hazel Lavery wrote: 'She was an exceptional character in every way – in addition to her beauty and kindness and charm of character she was extremely well endowed mentally – a thing she generally managed to conceal. I loved her and shall always regret her loss', 26 August 1950 (copy in the author's collection).

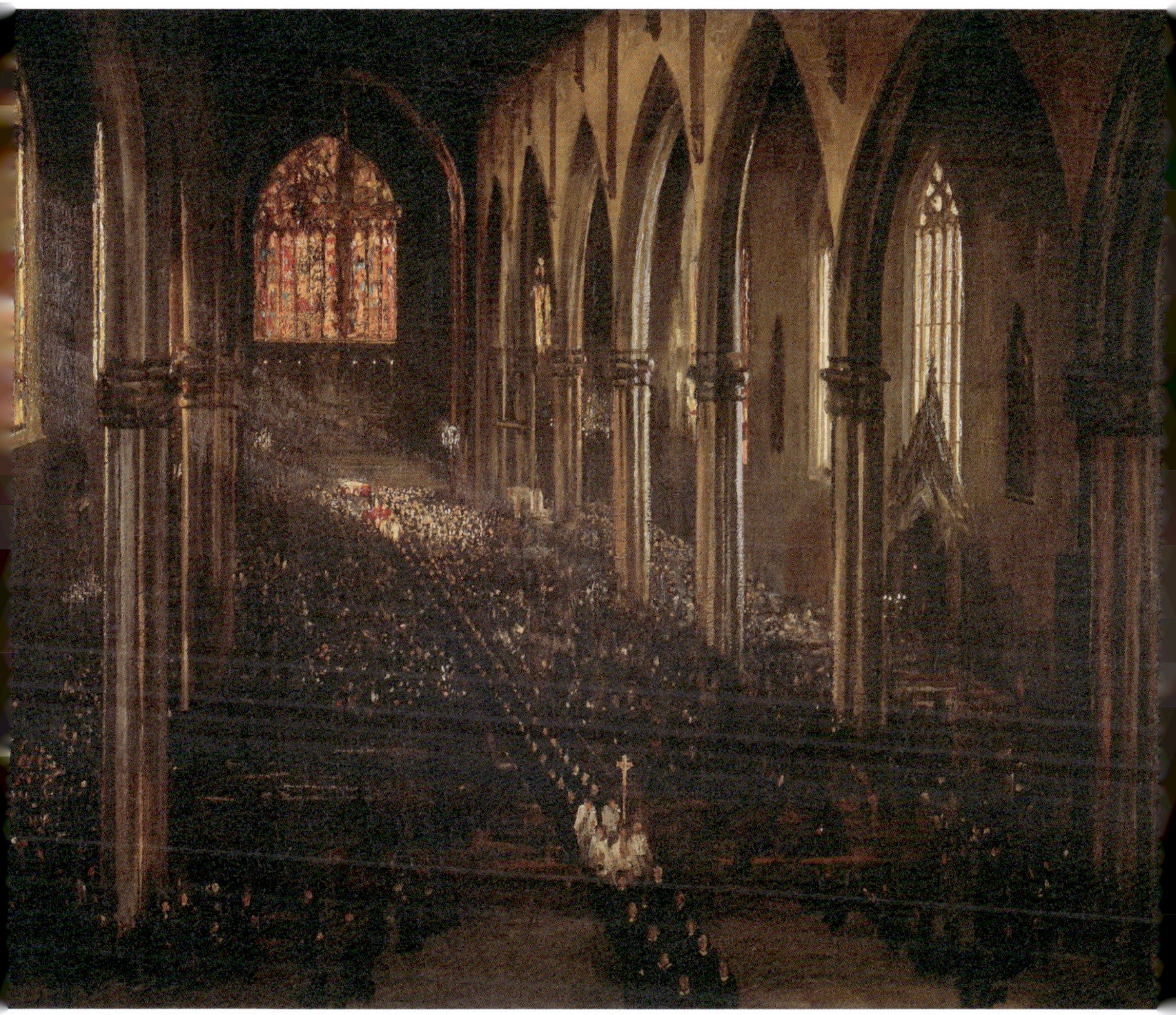

Southwark Cathedral, London, 1920
(Terence MacSwiney), 1920
Oil on canvas, 99 × 134.6 cm
Collection Dublin City Gallery The Hugh Lane

Collins did not travel to London as part of the Peace Delegation which was headed by Eamon De Valera[153] (who went by the title of President of the Irish Republic). On 16 July Eamon De Valera, Arthur Griffith and Count Plunkett visited the Laverys. The painter regretted that he was only given a couple of hours of the delegates' time. The negotiations were so short-lived that he only managed to get preliminary studies of De Valera and Arthur Griffith. The delegates returned to the Dáil with proposals which were rejected officially on 10 August.

A second delegation travelled to London in October; Eamon De Valera stayed in Ireland. The second delegation was led by Arthur Griffith, with Michael Collins, Robert Barton, Eamonn Duggan and Erskine Childers. On 11 October they met with the members of the English delegation including Lloyd George, Austin Chamberlain, Lord Birkenhead and Winston Churchill. It was Lavery's intention to make a painting of the signing of the Treaty similar to his painting *The End*. In order to secure sittings during the gruelling negotiation schedule, Lavery said that he would be at the disposal of the delegates if they telephoned a day in advance. He had just become a Royal Academician, so this offer meant that he was putting off paying clients. The Laverys also sent invitations to their joint exhibition at the Alpine Club Gallery. Churchill had written the foreword for their exhibition catalogue. The glamorous image of the couple by E.O. Hoppé used as the frontispiece of their catalogue belied their advancing years. Hazel had successfully maintained her looks, and was as much in demand as ever as an artist's model. One of her 1921 sittings was for the Italian sculptor, Eleuterio Riccardi, then living in London.

The Laverys now had unique access to the delegation, with the exception of Erskine Childers, who refused to have his portrait painted or to attend any dinners. In addition to the portrait painting, the Laverys attempted a diplomatic role. The artist himself wrote that he decided to make his studio 'a neutral ground where both sides might meet'.[154] Oliver St John Gogarty wrote in his memoir: 'Dinner at the

153 Eamon De Valera was a leader in the 1916 Rising. He was not executed because he was a citizen of the United States of America. He was elected President of Sinn Féin and spent the duration of the War of Independence in the United States of America seeking international approval for the cause of Irish Independence.

154 Lavery, *Life*, p. 208.

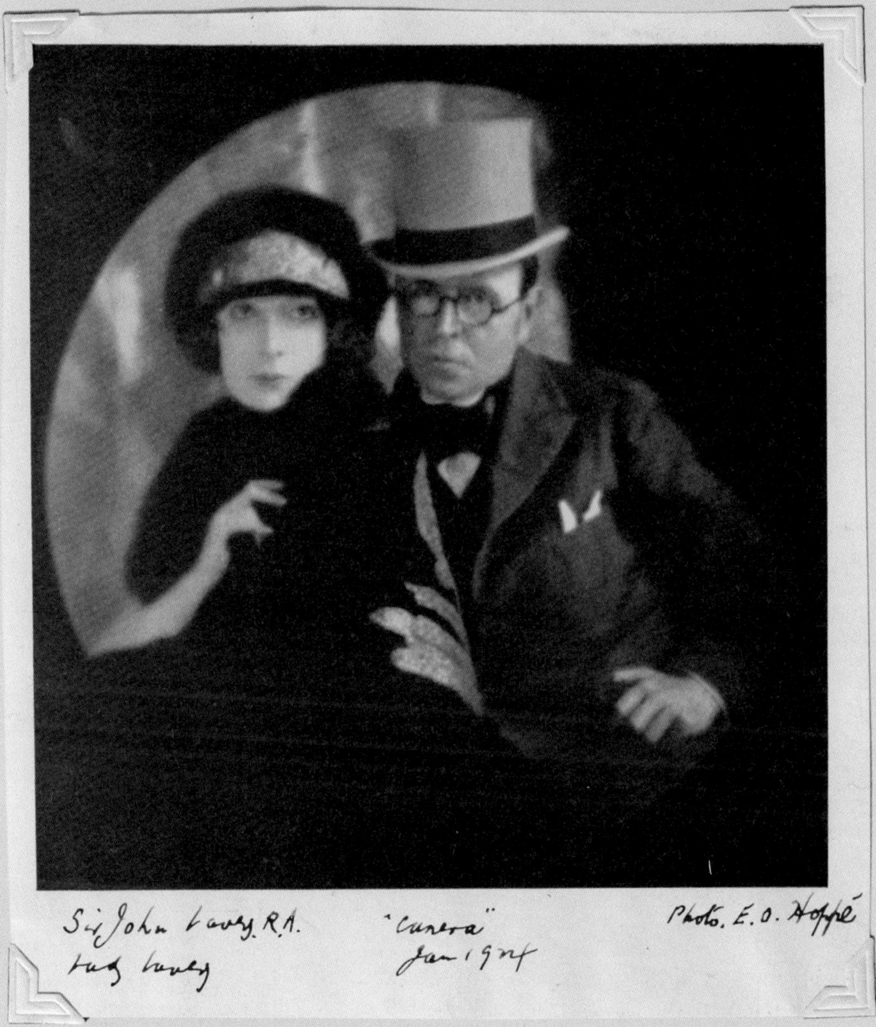

E.O. Hoppé: *Hazel, Lady Lavery, and Sir John Lavery*, 1922, reproduced in *Camera*, January 1924
The image was used as the frontispiece in the catalogue to their joint exhibition at the Alpine Club Gallery, London, October 1921.
Dublin City Gallery The Hugh Lane Archive

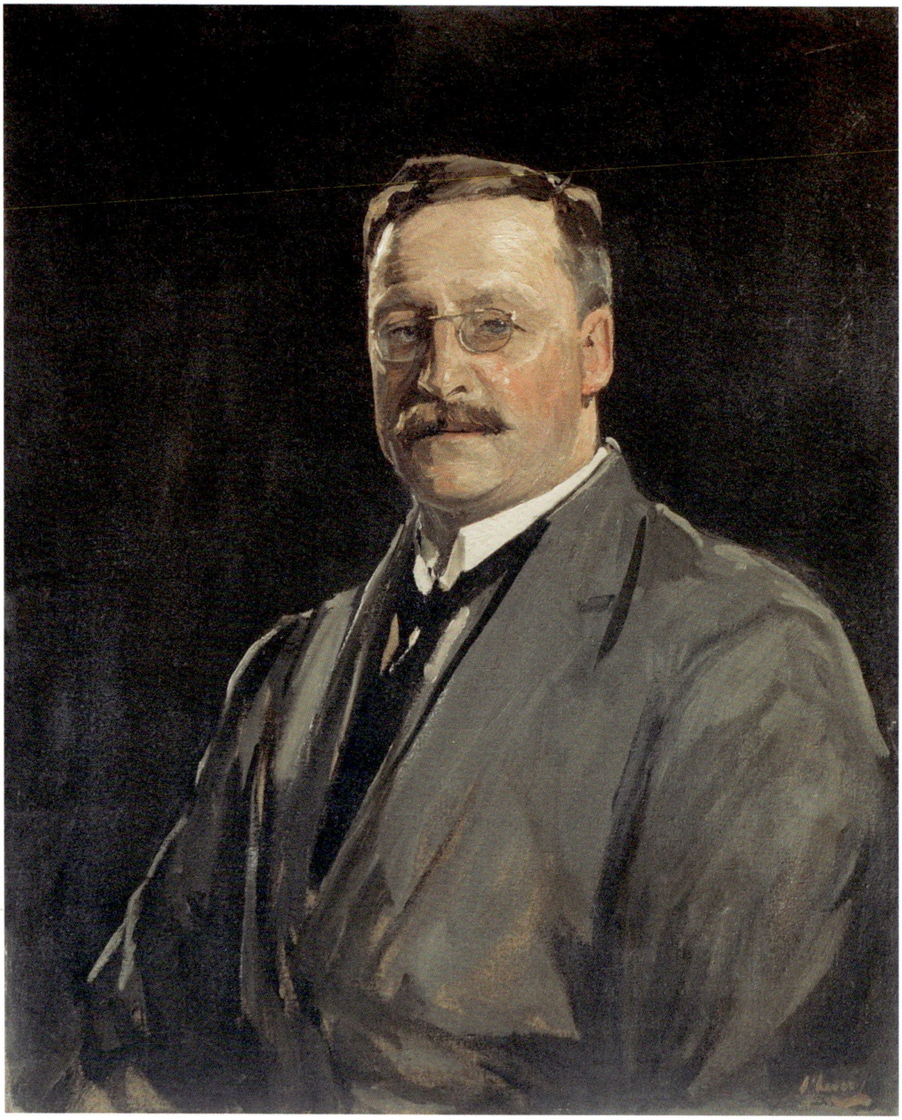

Arthur Griffith, 1921
Oil on canvas, 76.9 × 63.9 cm
Collection Dublin City Gallery The Hugh Lane

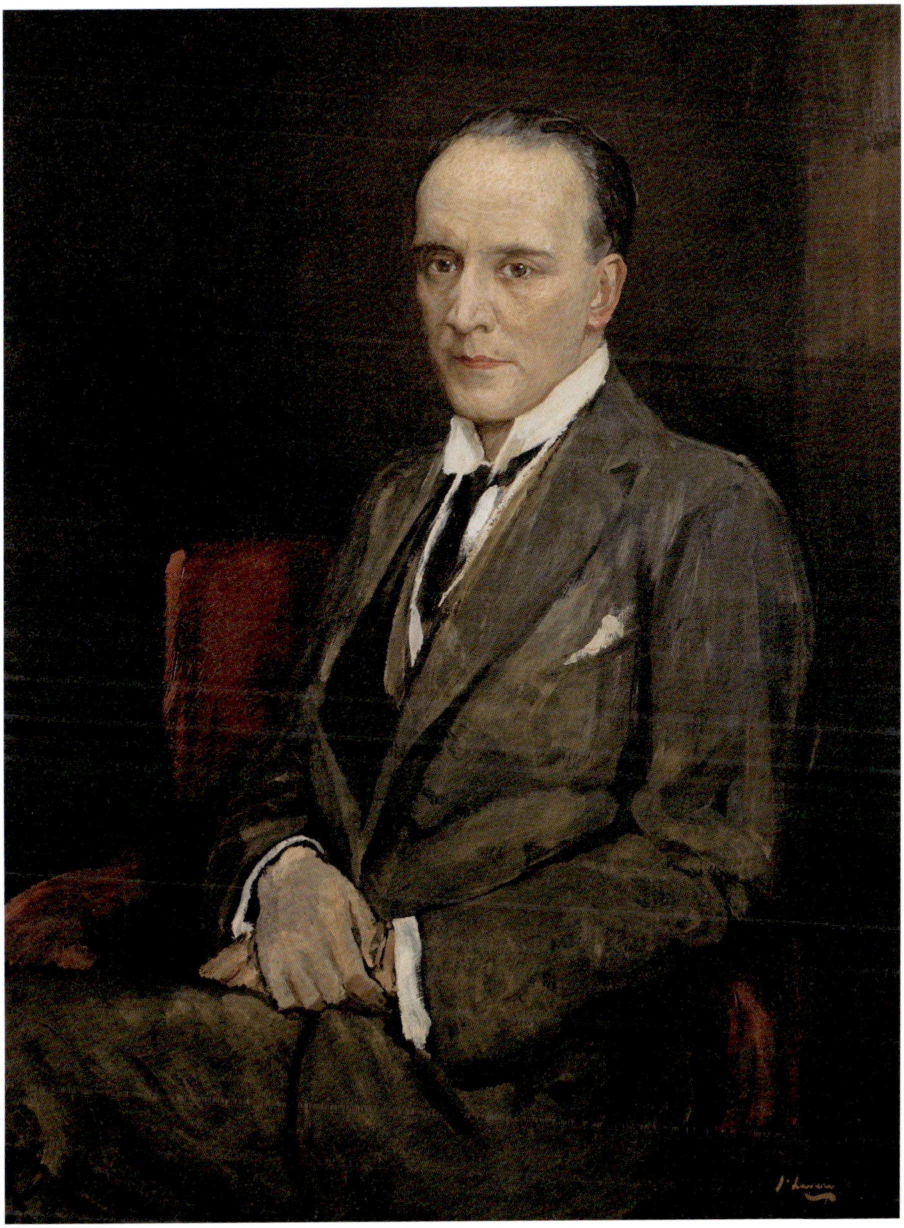

Kevin O'Higgins, 1923
Oil on board, 101.6 × 76.2 cm
Collection Dublin City Gallery The Hugh Lane

Laverys' brought you into the company of persons of incalculable importance. A house which was welcomed as an unofficial meeting place for rebel and ruler was of inestimable use and service to both sides – Ireland and England ... at 5 Cromwell Place men could meet as humans beyond the scent of herded wolves ... The Laverys did more to bring about a settlement than all the weary official and overlooked weeks at Hans Place'.[155]

Lavery never did get his painting of the signing of the Anglo-Irish Treaty; instead he had to content himself with the scene of the Ratification of the Treaty as it was passed in the House of Lords on 6 December 1921. The finished work, *Earl Morley Addressing the House of Lords*, is in the collection of Culture and Sport Glasgow (Museums).[156]

On 7 January 1922 members of Dáil Éireann voted 64 in favour and 58 against the acceptance of the terms of the Treaty. As a result of this legislation the island of Ireland was divided into two new entities – the self-governing Irish Free State with Dominion Status within the British Empire and the Province of Northern Ireland, which remained governed by Westminster. A provisional government was formed in Dublin with Michael Collins, Arthur Griffith, W.T. Cosgrave, Kevin O'Higgins and Eamon Duggan, among others, in the cabinet. The establishment of the Irish Army followed, and within months Lavery recorded the solemnity of *The Blessing of the Colours*, 1923.[157] This large canvas depicts a solemn moment, a soldier kneeling as the Archbishop (probably Dr Edward Byrne) confers a blessing on the tricolour.

Opposition to the Treaty in Ireland intensified in the early months of 1922 and those opposed were arming and preparing to use force. They became known as the Irregulars. Collins and others attended meetings in the Laverys' house[158] as the terms of the Treaty were being implemented. Kevin O'Higgins was one of those Irish ministers who attended many of these meetings in London. He described the Laverys as 'fine folks', but said that he disliked 'wooden men and painted women'.[159]

155 Oliver St John Gogarty, *As I was Going Down Sackville Street*, London, 1980, p.248.

156 The National Gallery of Ireland has a preparatory sketch of this work.

157 This painting is also known as *A Revolutionary Soldier Waiting to be Blessed*. The inscription on the reverse of the canvas reads, 'Blessing of the Colours of the Irish Free State'. The Crawford Gallery of Cork has the study of this work.

158 Hazel kept a list of meetings held in her home, but no details of those who attended or what was discussed.

159 Kevin O'Higgins to Bridie O'Higgins, undated, 1922, quoted in Sinéad Nic Cumhaill, *Lady Lavery, Her Salon and its Role in the Emergence of the Irish Free State*, University College Dublin, 1991, p.70.

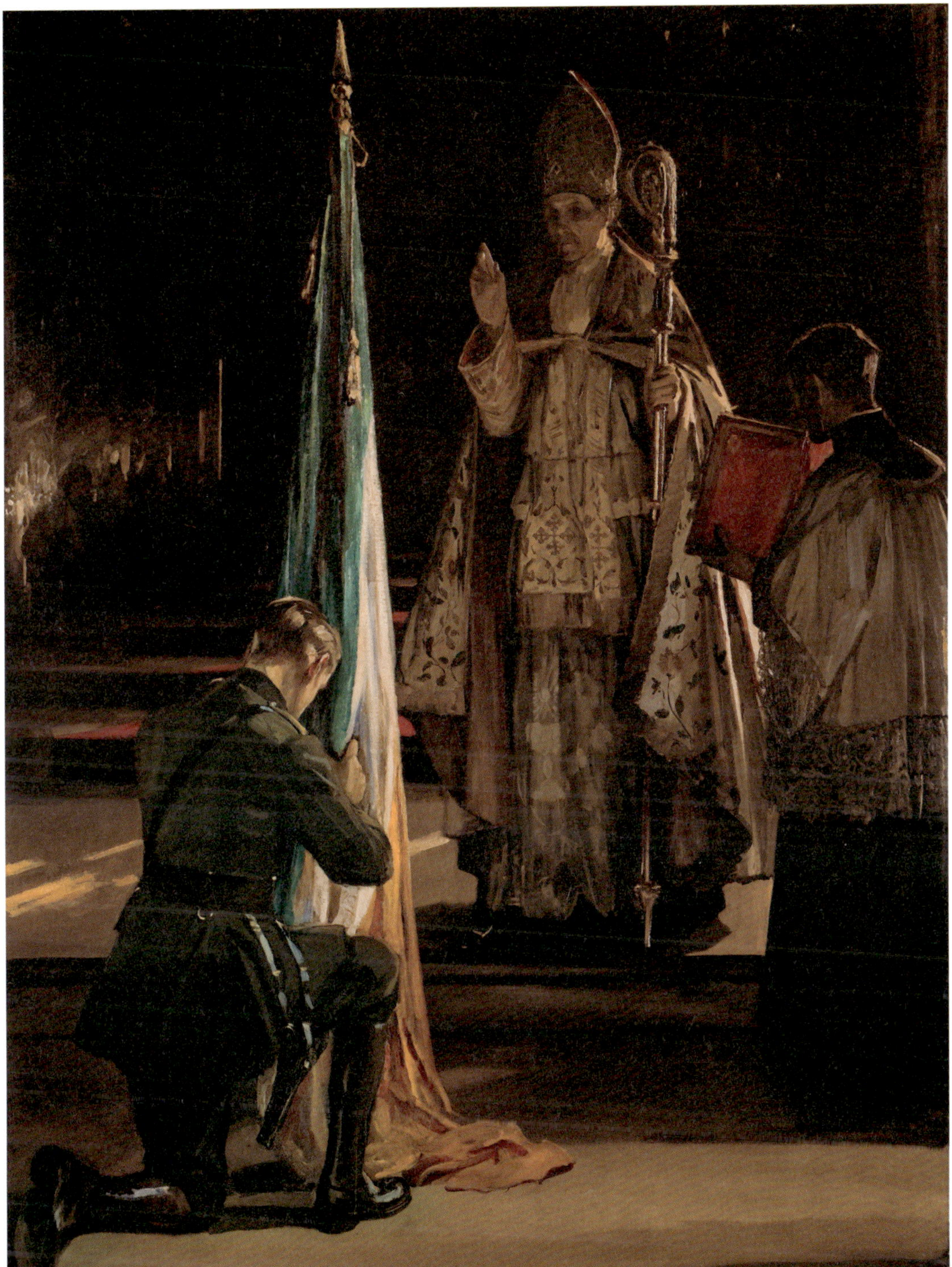

The Blessing of the Colours, 1922
Oil on canvas, 243.8 × 182.9 cm
Collection Dublin City Gallery The Hugh Lane

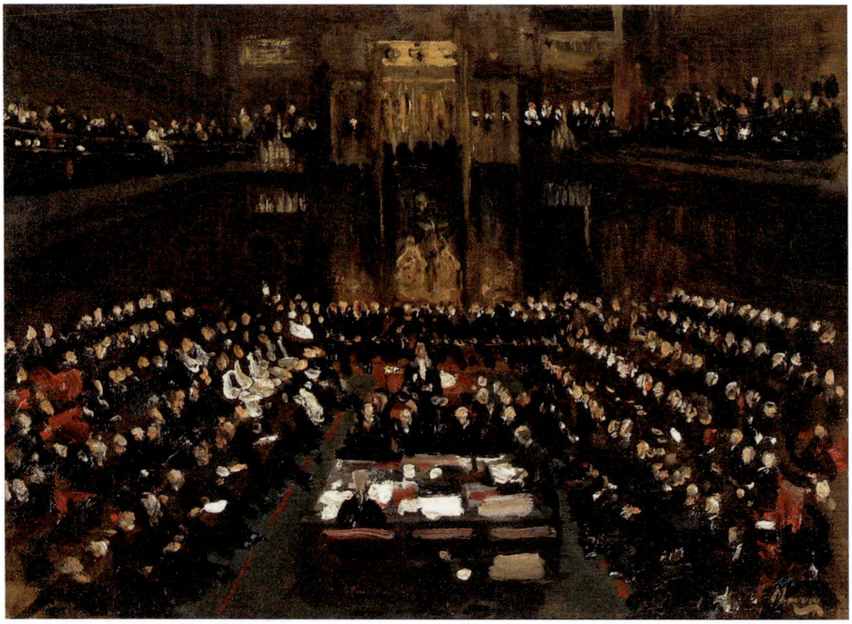

Sketch of the House of Lords in Session,
15 December 1921, 1921
Oil on artists' canvas-board, 25.5 × 36 cm
Courtesy of Pyms Gallery, London

Earl Morley Addressing the House of Lords, 1921–1922
Oil on canvas, 127 × 101.6 cm
Culture and Sport Glasgow (Museums)

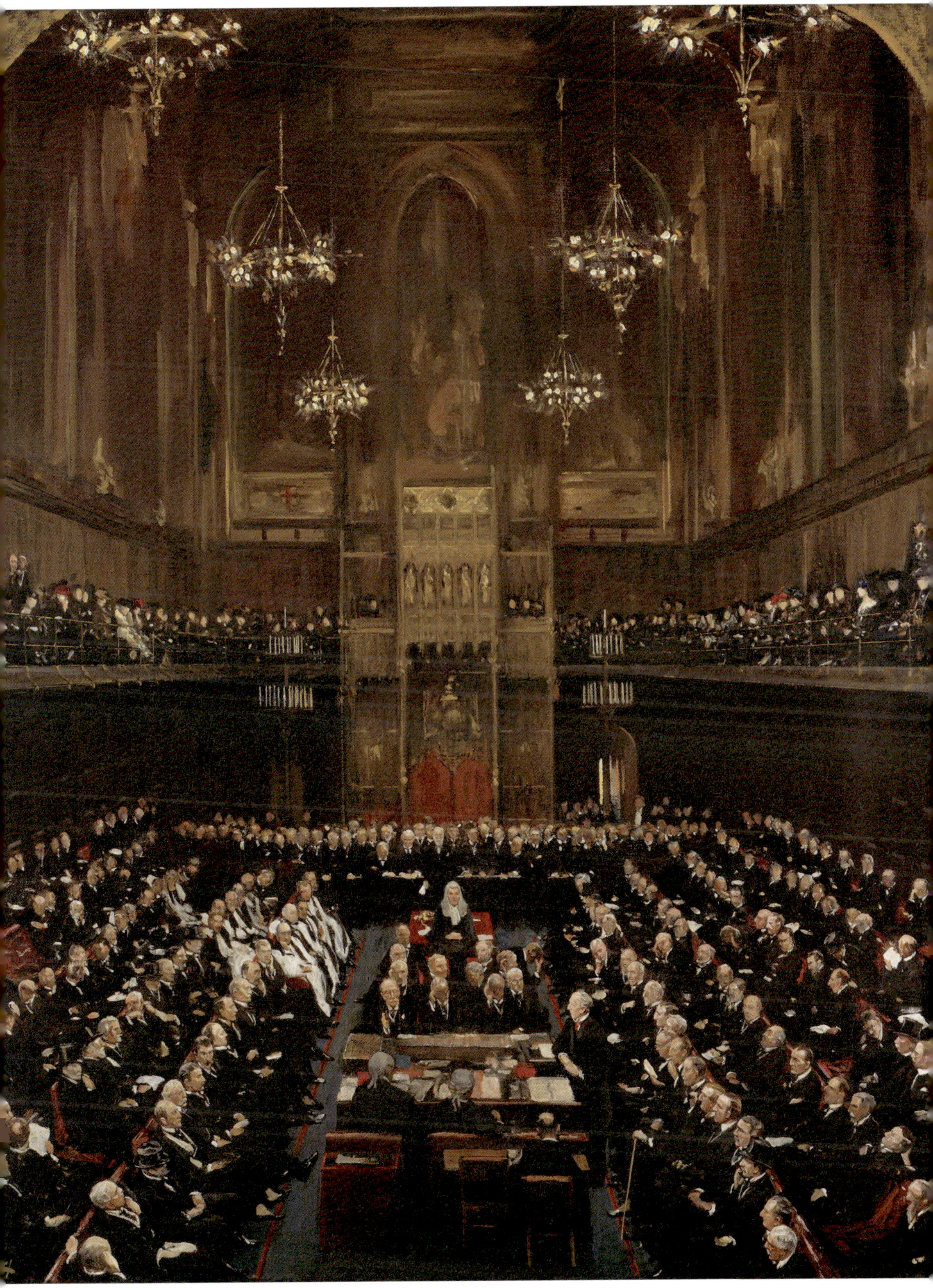

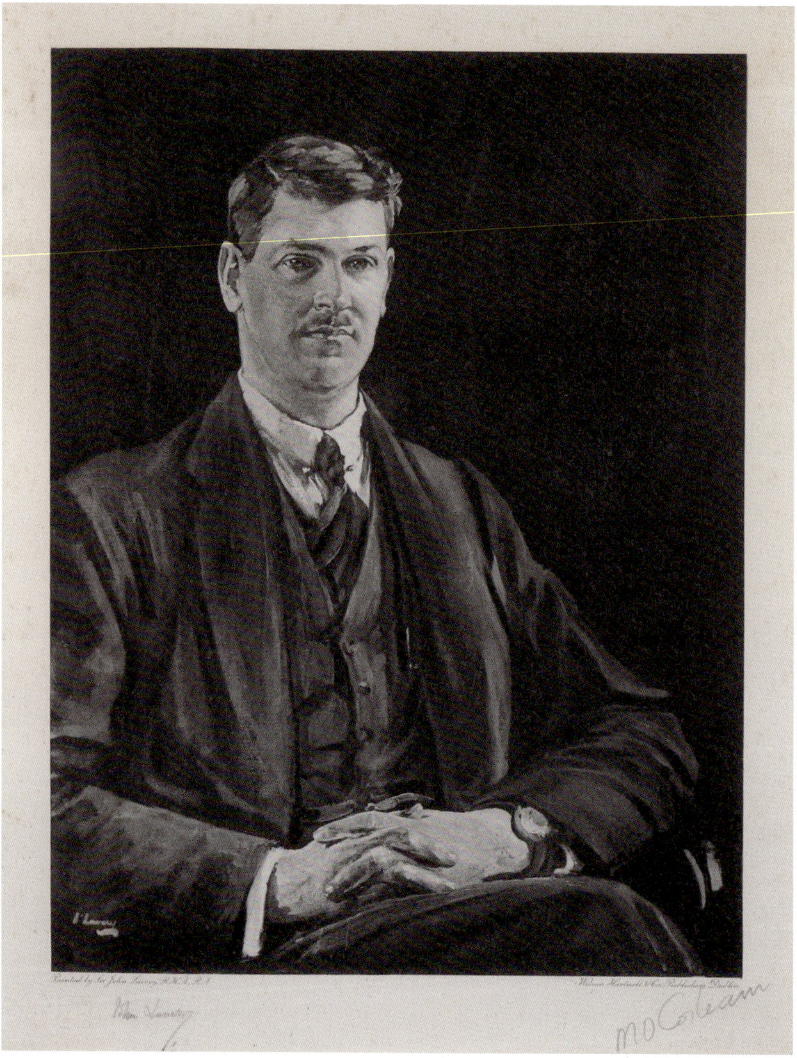

Lithograph of *Michael Collins (with his 'moustache' disguise)*, 1921
Published by Wilson Hartnell & Co., Dublin, 51 × 41 cm
Jackie Clarke Library and Archive, Ballina

160 Listed in Lady Lavery Scrapbook (private collection).

161 Hugh Kennedy to John Lavery, 1 July 1922, quoted in McCoole, *Hazel*, p. 93.

162 She wrote to Emmet Dalton later: 'The most violent of my correspondents (anonymous of course) concern themselves chiefly with the last week in Ireland August 16th to 20th and my meetings with Michael. Their information is perfectly accurate and they speak of the great danger I was in which of course I realised', 22 November 1922 (National Library of Ireland, MS 46,687).

Hazel Lavery's letters were used as an informal channel for communications with the British Cabinet. During June she set up a series of meetings for Collins with key politicians and civil servants at 5 Cromwell Place.[160]

Meanwhile, in Ireland the provisional government forces attacked Irregulars who had occupied key buildings in Dublin. On 30 June the Four Courts was in flames and those occupying it had been arrested. Lavery wanted to travel to Dublin to paint the scene. He was advised against it. The message to him read: 'Nothing spectacular now, street fighting and sniping with considerable danger to civilians.'[161] However, the Laverys did travel to Ireland, arriving in August, the day after Arthur Griffith had died suddenly. It had been suggested that they might stay in the vacant Viceregal Lodge, but they declined the invitation. They spent a considerable amount of time with Collins during the first week of their stay. Hazel was in his car when it was attacked by Anti-Treaty forces[162] and when Michael Collins was dining with them at the Royal Marine Hotel in Dun Laoghaire, a sniper was caught in the grounds of the hotel. Hazel and Lavery were also targets of attacks.

Collins had declared that he had signed his death warrant when he put his name to the Anglo-Irish Treaty. In July 1922 he assumed the role as Commander-in-Chief of the Irish Free State Army. While he was touring his home county of Cork, where there was intense opposition to the Treaty, he was ambushed and shot dead. The whole country mourned. Hazel, who had had a premonition that he would be killed, was distraught. A closeness had developed between her and Collins and he had a letter from Hazel on his body when he died.[163] She mourned publicly, saying she would wear widow's weeds to his funeral,[164] but she was dissuaded from doing so, out of respect to Collins' fiancée, Kitty Kiernan. Lavery was sensitive to Kitty's plight and gave her his painting,[165] *Michael Collins (with his 'moustache' disguise)*.[166] He then set about painting Collins lying in state which he called *Love of Ireland*:

163 It was returned to her covered in his blood. Sir Shane Leslie had the letter in the 1950s. It was his widow who donated it to the Kilmainham Jail Restoration Society. This letter is now in Kilmainham Gaol Museum.

164 Many women were linked to Michael Collins. Moya Llewelyn Davies, rumoured to be his lover, wrote of him: 'He was intensely shy, had no experience of women, and the drink rollicking Kiernan girls were easy company. I believe he never had any sexual experience. I got the impression that he was still virginal.' Moya Llewelyn Davies to P.S. O'Hegarty, 28 May 1943, (National Library of Ireland, MS 41,780). *Beloved Enemy*, the film of 1936, is said to have been based on the relationship between Lady Lavery and Michael Collins.

165 This painting was kept on an easel in Kitty Kiernan's sitting room until one day, sometime in the 1950s, it disappeared. No trace of this work has come to light since. Lithographs of Collins and Griffith were reproduced, including ones that were signed by the sitter and the artist. Others were reproduced after August 1922 as memorial issues, as both Collins and Griffith died in the same month.

166 Lavery chose to break up his collection of paintings of the Treaty delegates; his reason for this is undocumented. When he presented the collection to the Municipal Gallery in 1935 he had painted a replacement image of Michael Collins without the moustache he had grown (as a disguise) during the Treaty negotiations.

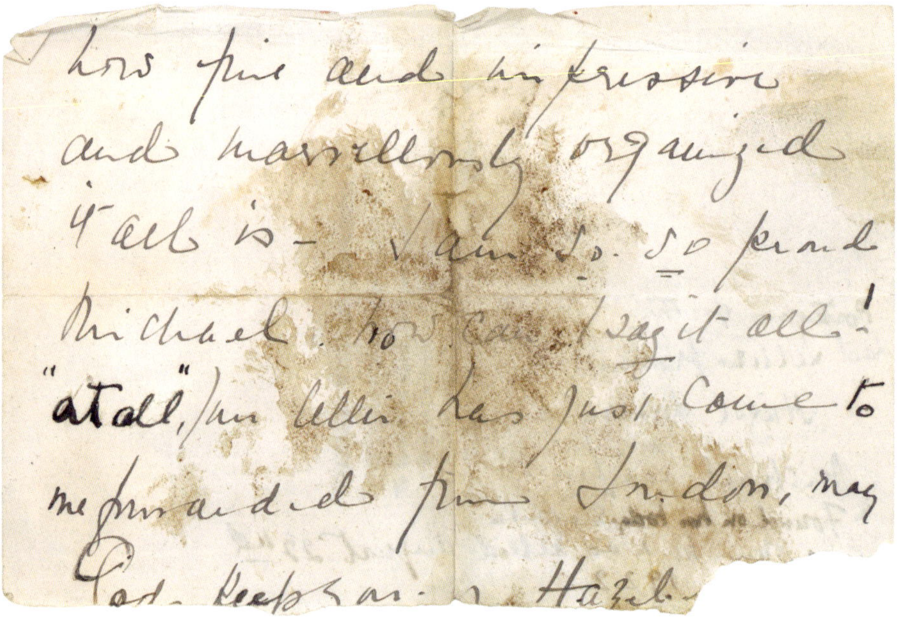

how fine and impressive
and marvellously organized
it all is – I am so so proud
Michael how can I say it all!
"at all", your letter has just come to
me forwarded from London, may
God keep you – Hazel

Blood stained letter written by Lady Lavery
in a book of Rosetti's poems taken from
Michael Collins' body after his death
Courtesy of Kilmainham Gaol Museum

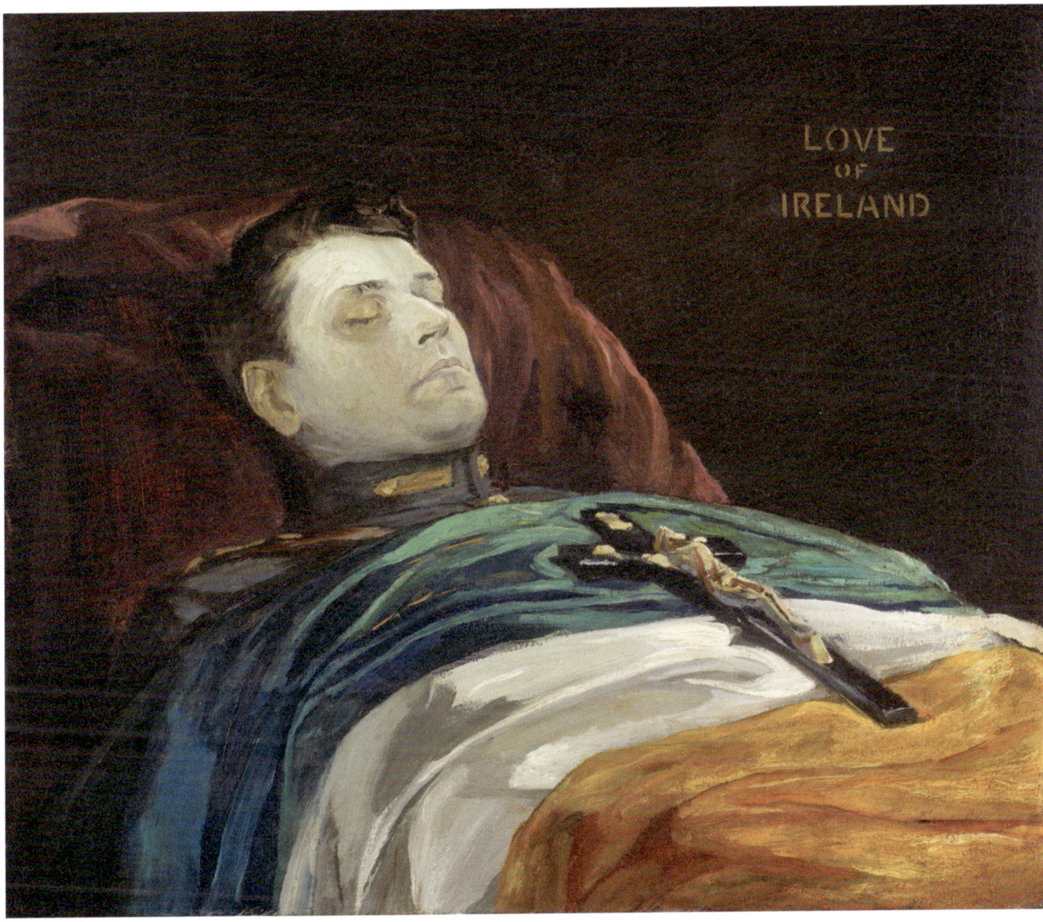

Michael Collins (Love of Ireland), 1922
Oil on canvas, 63.8 × 76.8 cm
Collection Dublin City Gallery The Hugh Lane

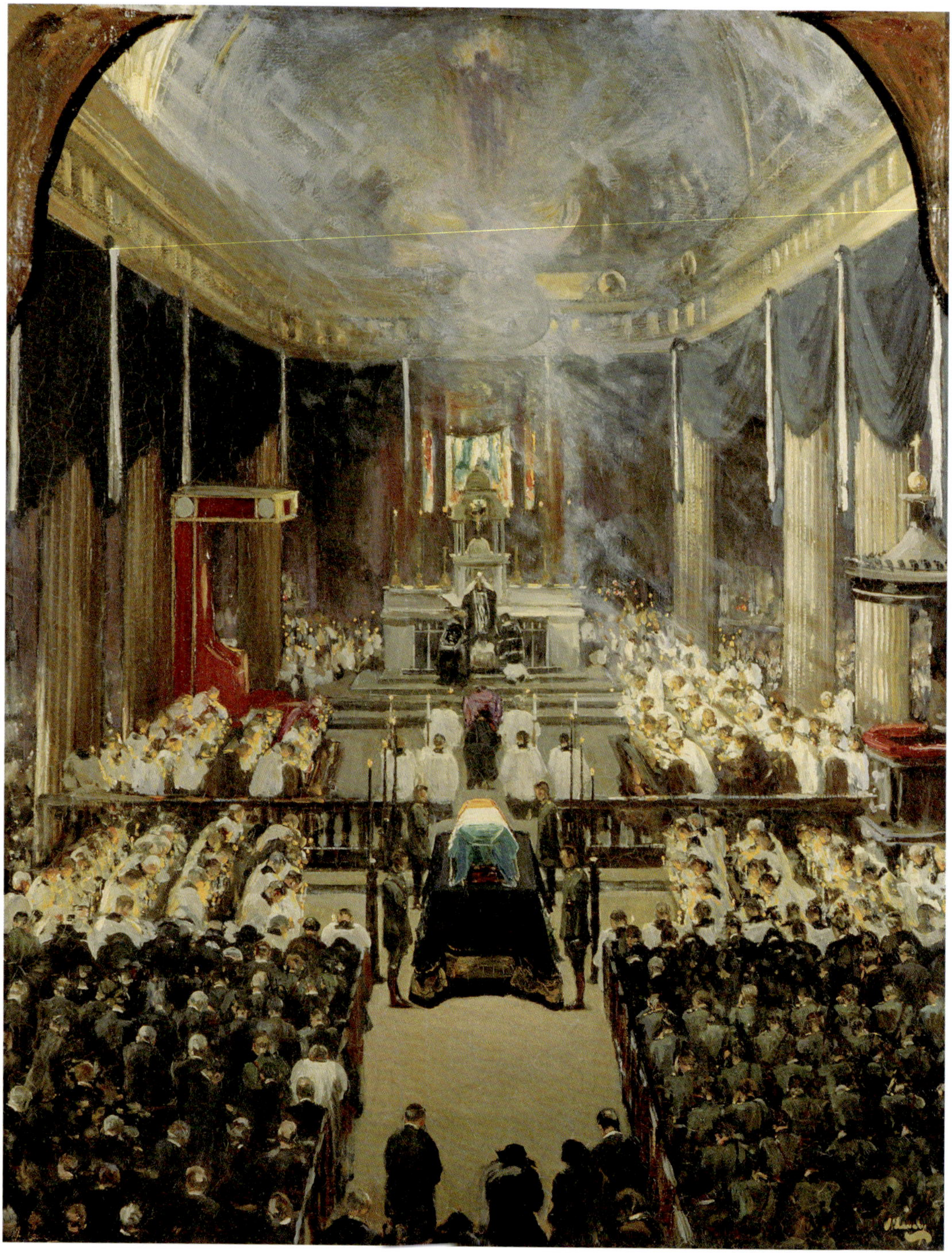

Pro-Cathedral, Dublin, 1922 (Michael Collins), 1922
Oil on canvas, 125.7 × 100.3 cm
Collection Dublin City Gallery The Hugh Lane

> 'I was allowed to paint him in death. Any grossness in his features, even the particular dent near the point of his nose, has disappeared. He might have been Napoleon in marble as he lay in his uniform ...'[167]

Lavery also recorded Collins' funeral from the balcony of Dublin's Pro-Cathedral. He also painted Collins' grave (untraced).

Throughout 1922 Lavery continued to get sittings for portraits on both sides of those who had negotiated the Treaty. He painted the Prime Minister of the Coalition Government, David Lloyd George. Lavery's sketchy style in this portrait is unusual, in contrast to his other more finished works. He also continued his Irish collection. He asked for and received a sitting with the Unionist leader Sir James Craig, the first Prime Minister of Northern Ireland. He painted Sir Edward Carson again, who accepted most graciously: 'I shall with pleasure comply with the wishes ... and agree the morning is the best time'.[168] Ever the wit, Carson called it 'Carson after the surrender',[169] which referred to the fact that Ireland was now partitioned, which had never been his intention. He had been campaigning for the whole of Ireland to stay in the union. He did not support the Government of Ireland Act and the Anglo-Irish Treaty, seeing them as a betrayal of the Southern Unionists.

The Civil War made setting up the Irish Free State even more difficult and put an acute strain on Anglo-Irish relations. The new government ordered mass arrests and executions throughout 1923 in a bid to bring to an end the resistance by Anti-Treaty forces. In December 1922 W.T. Cosgrave became the President of the Executive Council of the Irish Free State. However, Eamon De Valera refused to accept the authority of the Dáil and with his followers he created a shadow Republican government, which stayed in opposition to the formation of the new state in all its workings. In England a new Conservative government was formed

167 Lavery, *Life*, p. 217.
168 Sir Edward Carson to Sir John Lavery, July 7 1922 (Tate Archive, 7245.221).
169 Lavery, *Life*, p. 208.

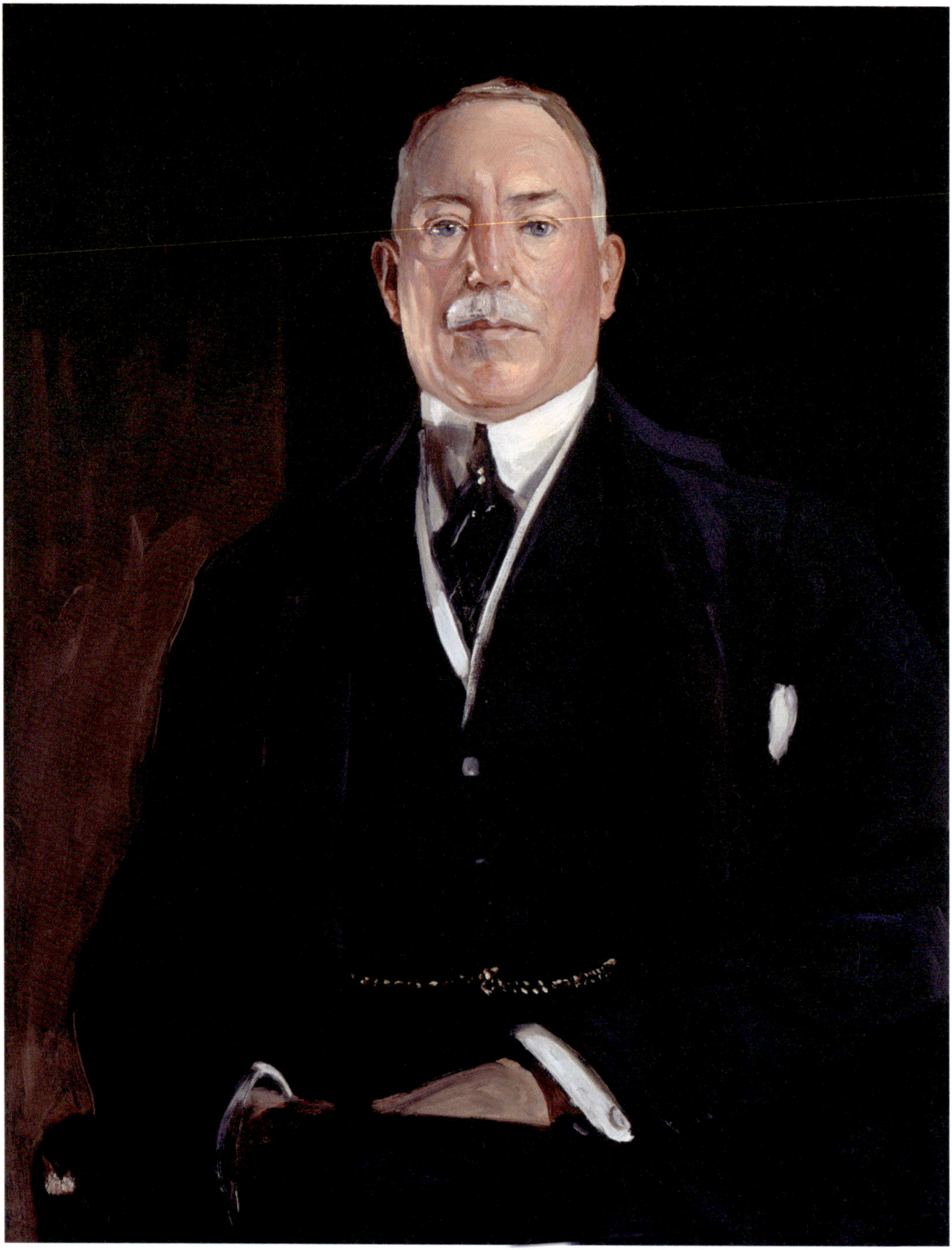

Rt. Hon. The Viscount Craigavon 1871–1940, First Prime Minister of Northern Ireland, 1923
Oil on canvas, 91.5 × 71.1 cm
Ulster Museum

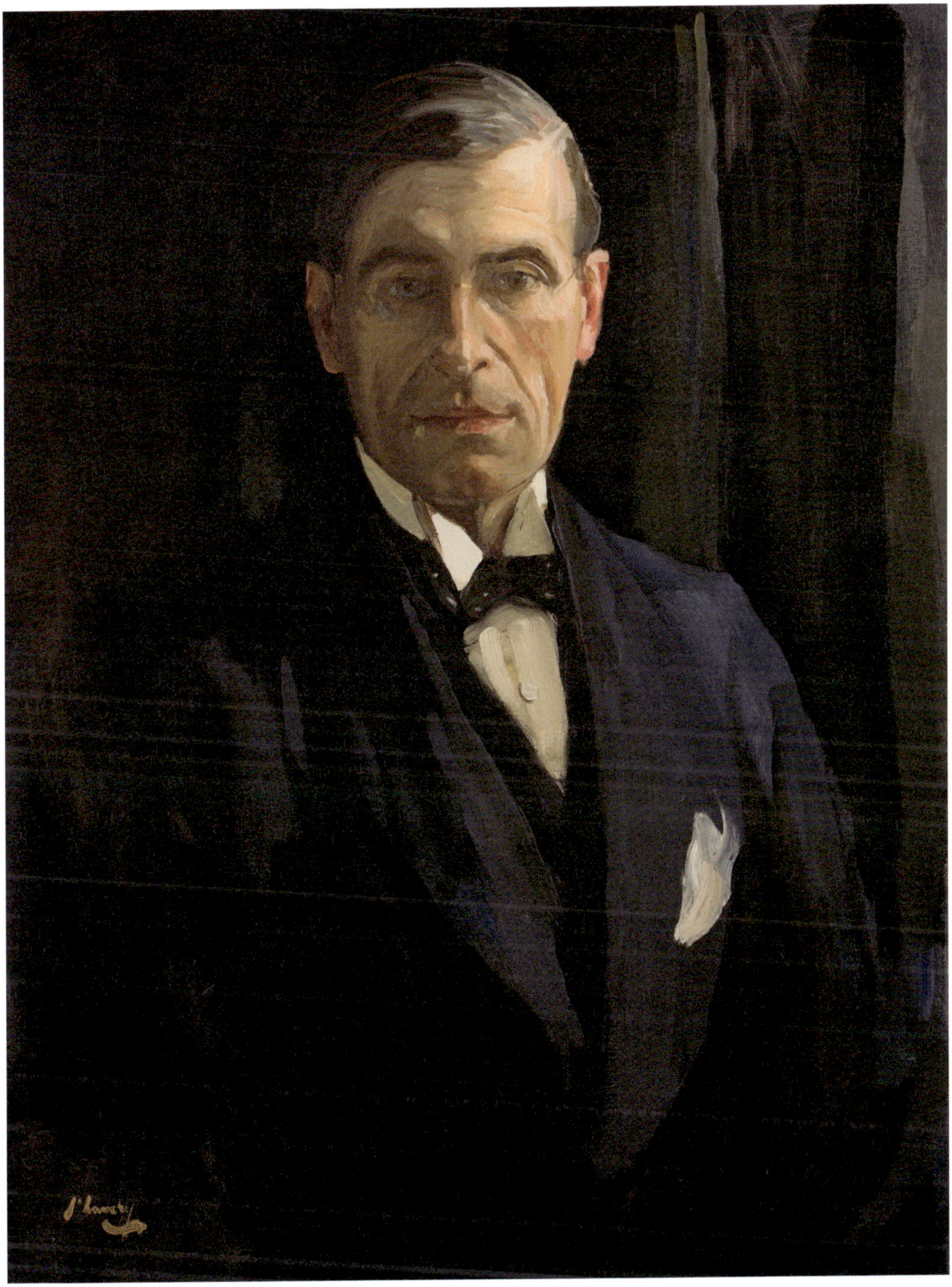

Sir Alfred Cope, 1925
Oil on canvas, 71.4 × 54.7 cm
Collection Dublin City Gallery The Hugh Lane

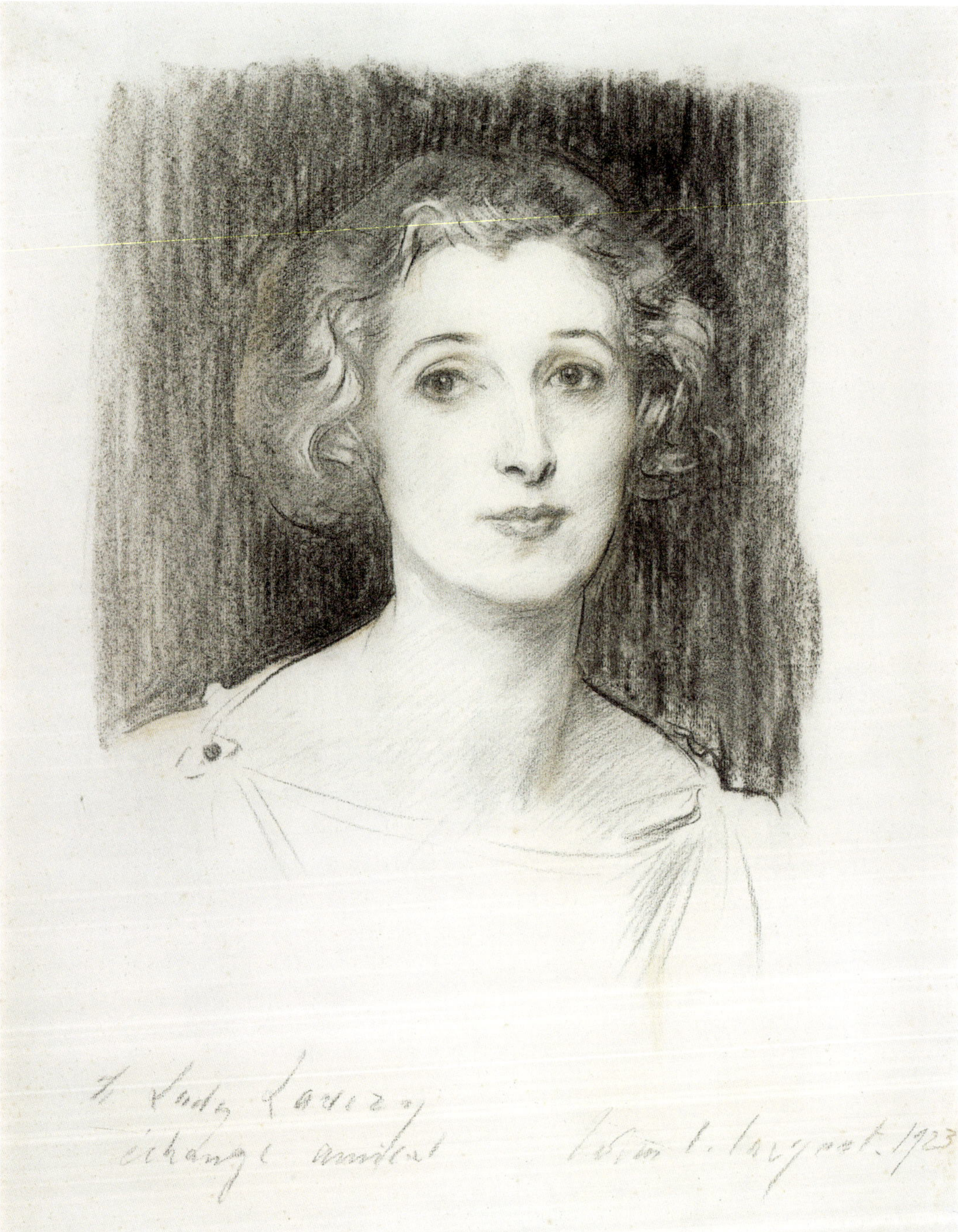

John Singer Sargent: *Lady Hazel Lavery (c. 1887–1935), 2nd Wife of the Artist, Sir John Lavery*, 1923
Charcoal on paper, 60 × 47 cm
Collection, National Gallery of Ireland

by Andrew Bonar Law, which had even less sympathy for Irish nationalism than the previous administration. The Laverys' home was used as a meeting place by a succession of Irish Free State ministers over the following years. The Irish Free State was a Dominion of the British Empire and it appointed a High Commissioner rather than an ambassador in London. The post was held by James MacNeill.[170] His wife Josephine recalled that while their home was the official headquarters 'Hazel's house was a most gracious centre of hospitality to the Irish political and artistic personalities,[171] and in the newspapers it was reported that at 5 Cromwell Place, 'the Kensington Studio of Sir John Lavery, the fashionable painter', 'the Free State has its official headquarters'.[172] The Laverys numbered among their friends the Irish writers George Bernard Shaw, Shane Leslie, Oliver St John Gogarty, Stephen Gwynn and his son Denis.[173] It was not exclusively an Irish set and included the Scottish writer J.M. Barrie, author of *Peter Pan*, and other international writers and artists. In 1923 John Singer Sargent was a regular visitor. He sketched Hazel (National Gallery of Ireland), capturing some of the sadness that many who met her saw in her.[174]

The door of Cromwell Place was open to British and Irish civil servants as well as to politicians. One of those was Alfred 'Andy' Cope,[175] Assistant Under Secretary for Ireland before Independence, who was introduced to the Laverys by Winston Churchill. He wrote to the Laverys in June 1923:

> 'I have closely watched the work you and Sir John have set out to accomplish ... You are two wonderful people carrying out in a wonderful way a most gigantic task ... This is indeed the most gigantic task, full of disappointments and perils for those who undertake it, and I speak from experience. It is a great task but it is a great goal, and though you and John may never see its accomplishment, yet you have taken it a long way towards the desired end ... I am convinced that antipathies can be removed and that you and John are travelling the only

170 James MacNeill had joined the Indian Civil Service in 1890 and later served in the West Indies and Fiji as an immigration investigator before returning to Ireland. He was Chairman of Dublin City Council in 1922 and brother of Eoin MacNeill, Chief of Staff of the Irish Volunteers.

171 Josephine MacNeill to Audrey Morris, 27 July 1951, quoted in McCoole, *Hazel*, p.109.

172 Unidentified press cutting, Lady Lavery Scrapbooks (private collection).

173 Denis Gwynn had been a pupil of P.H. Pearse, the leader of the 1916 Rising. He later became a Professor of History in University College Cork. He was the second husband of Hazel's daughter, Alice.

174 This charcoal sketch was given to the Laverys. Sargent wrote on it '*échange amical*'. The exchange was for John Lavery's *Joe Childs, Rothschild's Jockey*, inscribed by the artist 'to John Sargent from John Lavery, 1923'. I am grateful to Richard H. Finnegan for this reference.

175 Alfred W. Cope had worked in the Ministry of Pensions until 1920 when he was sent to Ireland. According to Margery Forester in *Michael Collins, The Lost Leader*, London, 1972, Cope 'was genuinely devoted to the task of winning peace for Ireland'. He assisted with the withdrawal of British troops in Ireland and received a knighthood in 1922. From 1922 to 1924 he was General Secretary of the British Liberal Party and gave private advice to the Irish Free State during a boundary dispute in 1925.

> road to remove them ... you and John can and must go on, for you are doing big things and power to do big things increases daily.'[176]

By the summer of 1923 Hazel had become intimate with Kevin O'Higgins,[177] now the Vice President of the Executive Council and Minister for Home Affairs. The Laverys were guests at his home in Dublin, and Hazel had attended the Royal Dublin Horse Show with O'Higgins and they sat together in the Royal Box. During their visit in 1923 the Laverys also stayed with Tim Healy, now the King's representative, the Governor General,[178] whose candidacy the Laverys had endorsed with the British government. Hazel also assisted Healy with the protocol required in the Viceregal Lodge. Lavery had been mentioned for the post of Governor General from 1922 but it was never to be. By 1926 the idea was gaining currency and had been promoted by Kevin O'Higgins.[179] As Hazel wrote to Lennox Robinson: 'I have heard the idea very seriously discussed, but I am afraid it will never happen, much as I would love it. John Lavery would be one to say it was 'out of the question' and absurd'. And Dubliners would object violently to such 'Aliens'. A Belfast knight and his Irish American lady would never be acceptable'.[180]

The Laverys' relationship with Ireland changed dramatically with the assassination of Kevin O'Higgins on 10 July 1927. O'Higgins was Minister of Justice during the years of the most draconian government measures of the Civil War. He was shot when he travelled to Mass unaccompanied by his usual bodyguard. Three Republicans randomly passing through the area chanced upon the unarmed minister and gunned him down. Hazel tried to maintain a diplomatic role after O'Higgins' death, which she did, with varying degrees of success.

James MacNeill, former Irish High Commissioner in London, was selected for the role of Governor General in February 1928. Hazel had been promoting the candidacy for Thomas Bodkin, another of her admirers, for this vacant position of

176 Andy Cope to Hazel Lavery, 30 June 1923, quoted in McCoole, *Hazel*, pp. 223–224.

177 According to Moya Llewelyn Davies, Frank Pakenham told her that Hazel Lavery 'told him she was in love with Mick, but not he with her and that Kevin O'Higgins was in love with her but not she with him. Even if she did say this – Pakenham's not reliable – it may just have been her vanity. But I know she haunted O'Higgins' office whenever he was in London.' Moya Llewelyn Davies to P.S. O'Hegarty, 8 June 1943, (National Library of Ireland, MS 41,780).

178 The post of Governor General existed in all the dominions of the British Empire, and was in accordance with the Irish Free State constitution.

179 By 1926 Alice was an almost permanent resident in County Kilkenny, having been brought there on a visit by a school friend. In 1930 she married Jack McEnery and moved to lived in Rossenarra House in Kilmoganny, a house reputed to have been designed by the architect of the White House in Washington, DC, James Hoban, who came from nearby Desart in Callan. Information supplied to the author by the Lady Lavery Society, Kilkenny.

180 Hazel Lavery to Lennox Robinson, November 1926, quoted in McCoole, *Hazel*, pp. 137–138.

High Commissioner in London. He did not get the job, but he was able to be of use to Hazel in his capacity as the Director the National Gallery of Ireland and appointee to the Currency Commission. Thomas Bodkin came up with the idea of using Hazel's image as the motif on the Irish banknotes. Bodkin brought two photographs to a meeting of the Currency Commission and proposed Lavery as the artist to produce 'a painting of a beautiful Irish type'.[181] When the official request was issued from Joseph Brennan it read: 'On protective and artistic grounds the use of a well engraved portrait has much to recommend it' and 'a beautiful female head treated in some emblematic fashion might perhaps have some Irish association'.[182] Lavery did not immediately accept the commission, suggesting that it go to open competition or that the Irish artist Seán Keating should be considered, as Lavery believed he was the ideal choice to design the notes. He was eventually persuaded, however, and he set about designing an image using his wife as model. Hazel wrote, disingenuously, that she thought it 'wildly improbable, unlikely, impracticable, unpopular, impossible! That any committee would fall in with such a suggestion'.[183] She delighted in spreading the news of this commission and leaked 'the truth' to the Irish papers, including supplying a recent studio photograph to highlight the likeness. This placed the Currency Commission and government in an embarrassing position, that this was an image of an actual living person, an American, with a British title, who had never lived in Ireland and was, moreover, the subject of persistent rumours of impropriety.[184] It became even more awkward when the full image, which Lavery called *Killarney*, was used on the larger denomination notes while the smaller denominations, those in main circulation, such as the £1 and 10 shilling note, had only the head. It appeared as if Lady Lavery had replaced the monarch on the Irish Free State banknotes.

181 Thomas Bodkin to Hazel Lavery, 21 December 1927, quoted in McCoole, *Hazel*, p. 140.

182 Joseph Brennan to John Lavery, 30 December 1927, quoted in McCoole, *Hazel*, p. 140.

183 Hazel Lavery to Thomas Bodkin, 26 December 1927, quoted in McCoole, *Hazel*, p. 141.

184 The discovery of her correspondence with Kevin O'Higgins, affected her reputation and friendships with the Irish cabinet and senior government officials. This appears to have affected even the National Gallery of Ireland's acceptance of Lavery's gift of paintings. See McCoole, *Hazel*, p. 136.

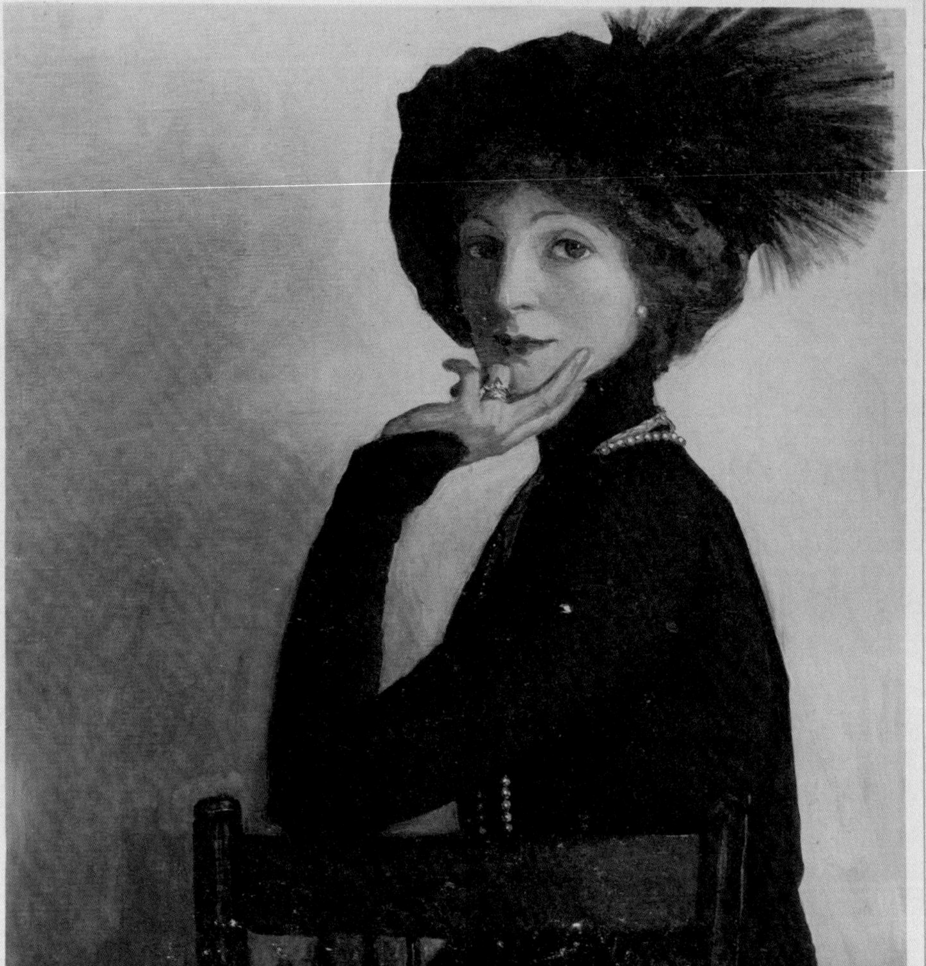

1909

30 × 25

Mrs. Lavery

This head with shawl and elbow resting on reversed was used for the Colleen on the Irish Free State notes.

The above picture is underneath.

J L

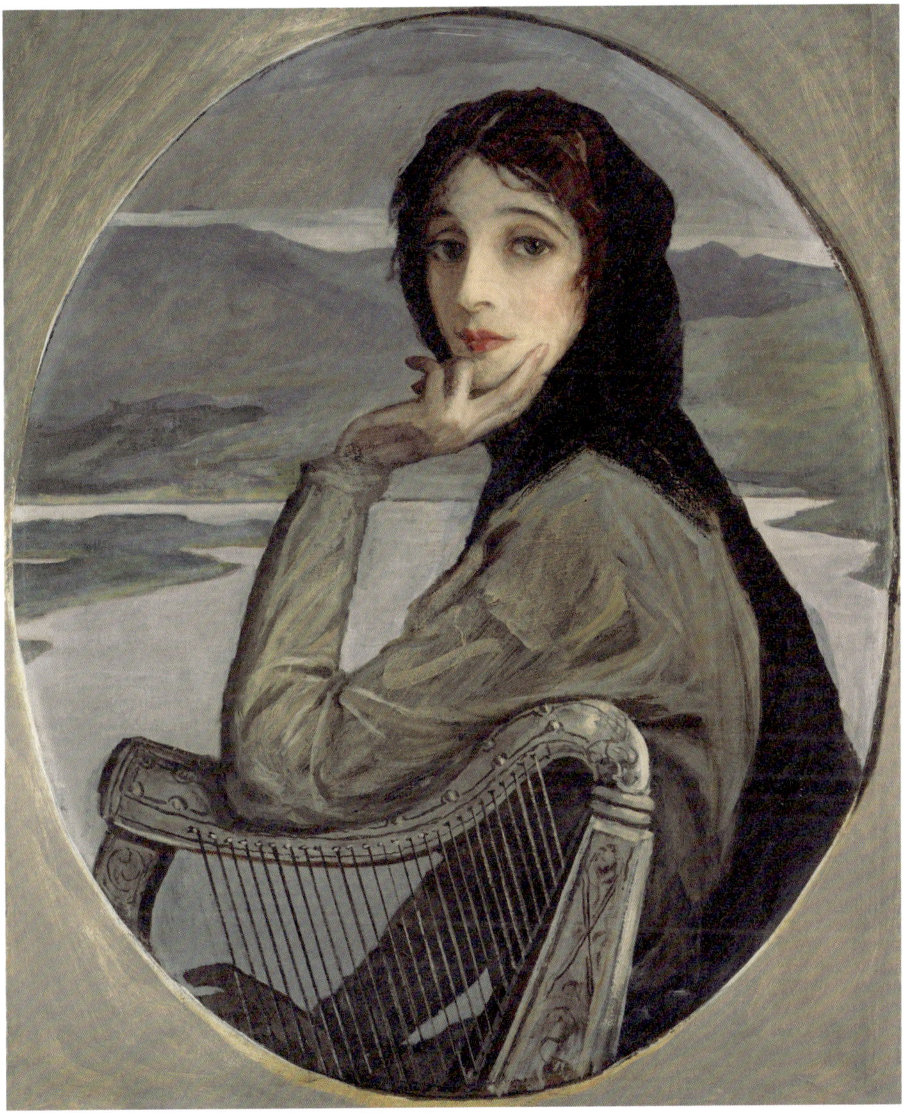

Photograph of *Mrs Lavery*, 1909
John Lavery Venice exhibition album, 1910
The inscription reads:
'This head with shaw [*sic*] and elbow resting on harp reversed was used for the Coleen on the Irish Free State notes.
The above picture is underneath.'
Dublin City Gallery The Hugh Lane Archive

Portrait of Lady Lavery as Kathleen Ni Houlihan, 1927
Oil on canvas, 75.5 × 62.5 cm
Collection, The Central Bank and Financial Services Authority of Ireland

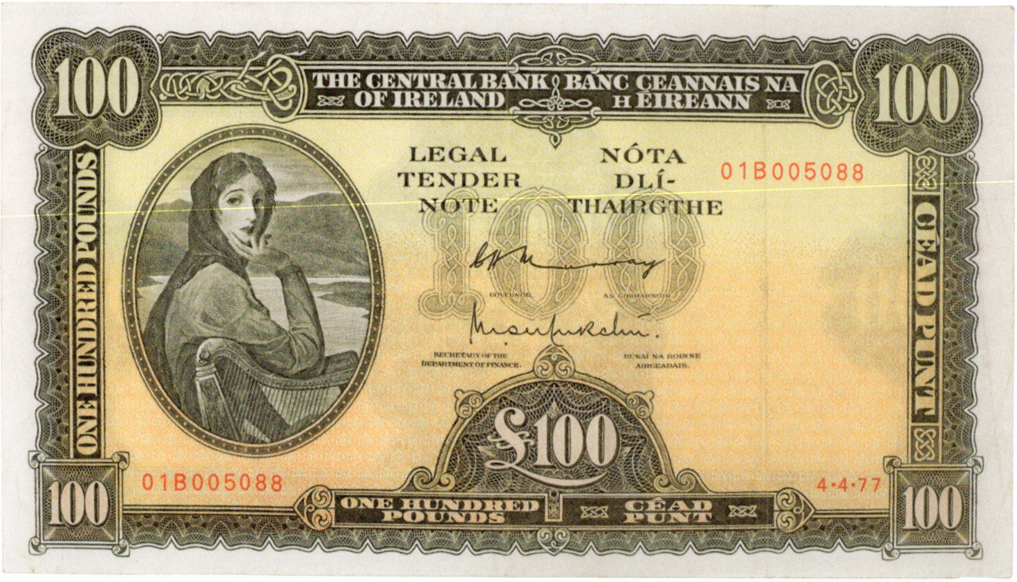

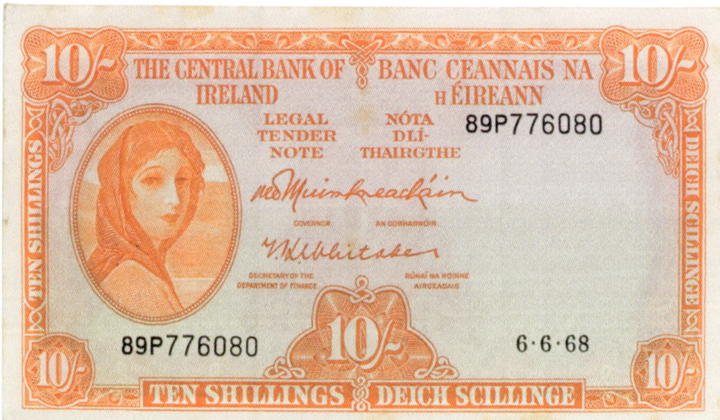

£100 Banknote (A Series). Date on first notes issued: 10·9·28; date on last notes: 4·4·77.

Private collection

10 Shilling Note (A Series). Date on first notes issued: 10·9·28; date on last notes: 6·6·68.

Private collection

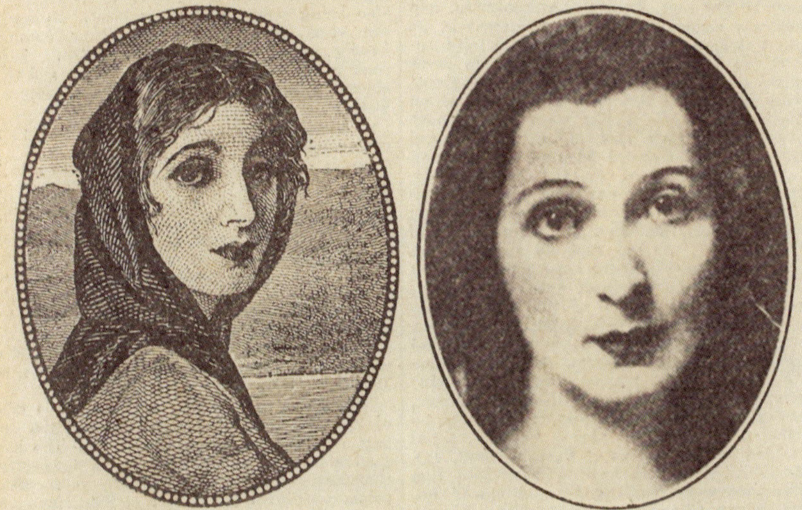

SIR JOHN LAVERY'S MODEL.—There is a striking resemblance between the Irish colleen on the new Free State notes and Lady Lavery. The Press Associa-tiontion states that it has the best authority for saying that Sir John Lavery's model was Lady Lavery. The picture on the left appears on the new notes and that on the right is from a recent photograph of Lady Lavery.

'Sir John Lavery's model', *The Irish Times*, 14 September 1928

Courtesy of the National Library of Ireland

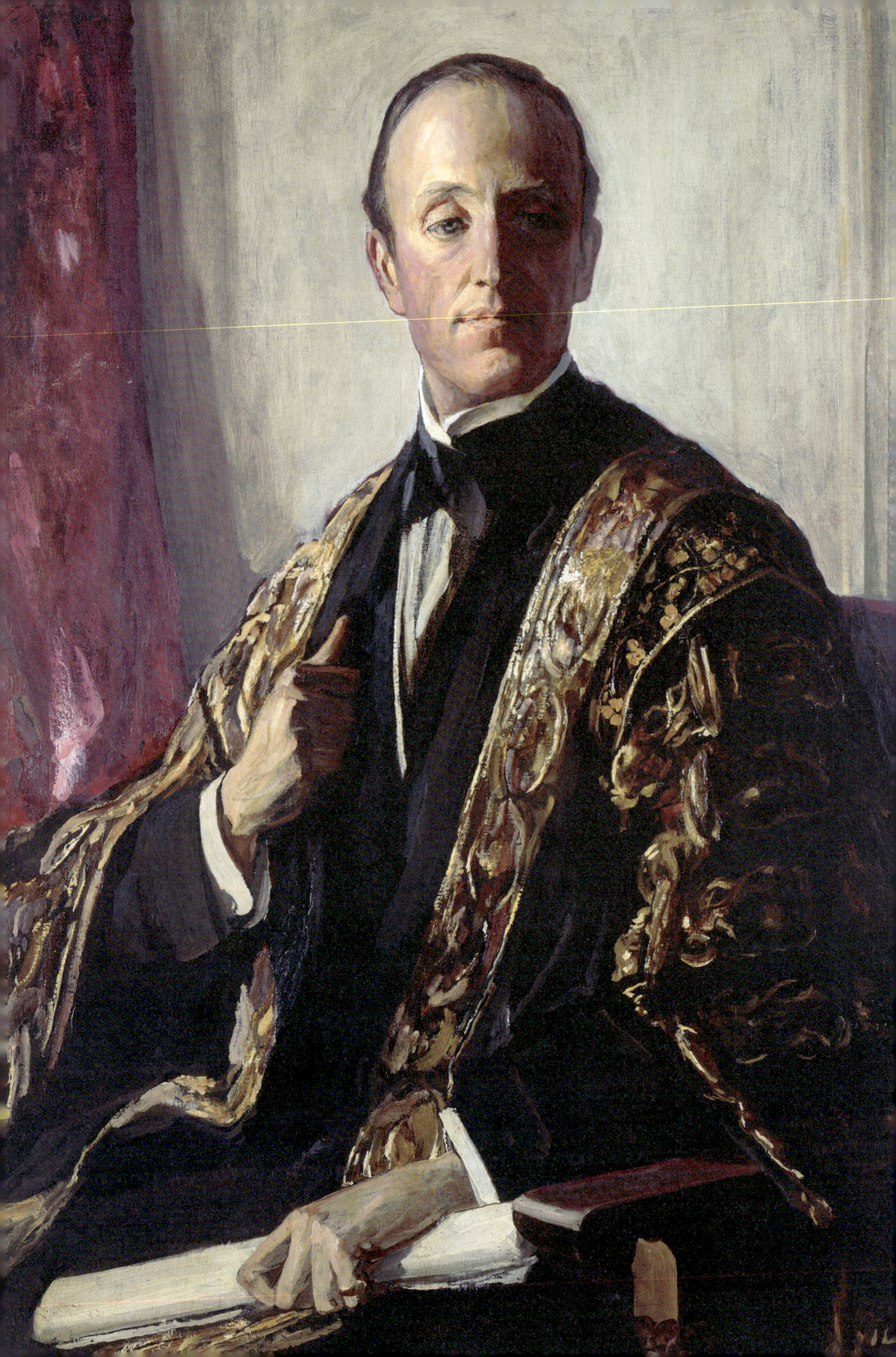

The Laverys travelled extensively in the North in 1928. They visited Mount Stewart, County Down, the home of Lord and Lady Londonderry. Their long time friend, Charlie, Marquess of Londonderry, assisted with the arrangements for the Church of Ireland archbishop, Charles D'Arcy, to sit for Lavery. The archbishop, who had served briefly as Archbishop of Dublin, was now Archbishop of Armagh and Primate of All Ireland. While Lavery was at Mount Stewart completing this portrait, he received a death threat by way of an anonymous letter with the lines: 'The Londonderry Air with its opening lines; I met murder by the way'. Hazel dismissed it with, 'Never mind, carry on', which they did.[185] During 1928 Lavery continued his collection of Irish portraits, including the Bishop of Down, Connor and Dromore, the Right Reverend Dr Charles Thornton Primrose Grierson, MA. Lavery selected the nationalist Joe Devlin MP to sit for him. When asked by Lavery what he thought of his portrait, Devlin described it as 'very ugly but it's very like me'.[186] The portraits of Sir Edward Archdale, Imperial Grand Master of the Orange Lodge, and Sir Joseph Davison, Grand Master of the Belfast Orangemen, were also completed at this time.

Eamon De Valera and his Republican followers of the newly formed Fianna Fáil party entered Dáil Éireann in 1927. A new identity was being forged for the Irish Free State and Hazel felt excluded, agreeing with Thomas Bodkin's assessment on 21 July 1928: 'The attitude of the Government towards England is sickening ... what can they expect to gain in honour or in profit by childishly irritating our neighbour, our best customer and our accepted ally ...'[187] In the North Hazel felt no more welcome: 'they are all kindness and attention personified, only somehow I can't bloom among them'.[188] Lavery continued to record his Ireland in paint. He depicted the Unionist marching tradition of the 12th of July parade at Portadown in 1928 and the following year went to the ancient Irish pilgrimage site at Lough Derg in County Donegal, where penitents walked in bare feet and fasted. Hazel, despite being a Catholic convert, opted to stay with the MacNeills[189] in

185 Lavery, *Life*, pp. 210–211.
186 T.J. Campbell, 'Fifty Years of Ulster', *Irish News*, 10 February 1941.
187 Thomas Bodkin to Hazel Lavery, 21 July 1928, quoted in McCoole, *Hazel*, p. 144.
188 Hazel Lavery to Thomas Bodkin, 8 August 1928, quoted in McCoole, *Hazel*, p. 145.

The Marquess of Londonderry, KG *1878–1949,*
Chancellor of The Queen's University of Belfast, c. 1924
Oil on canvas, 101.6 × 76.2 cm
Ulster Museum

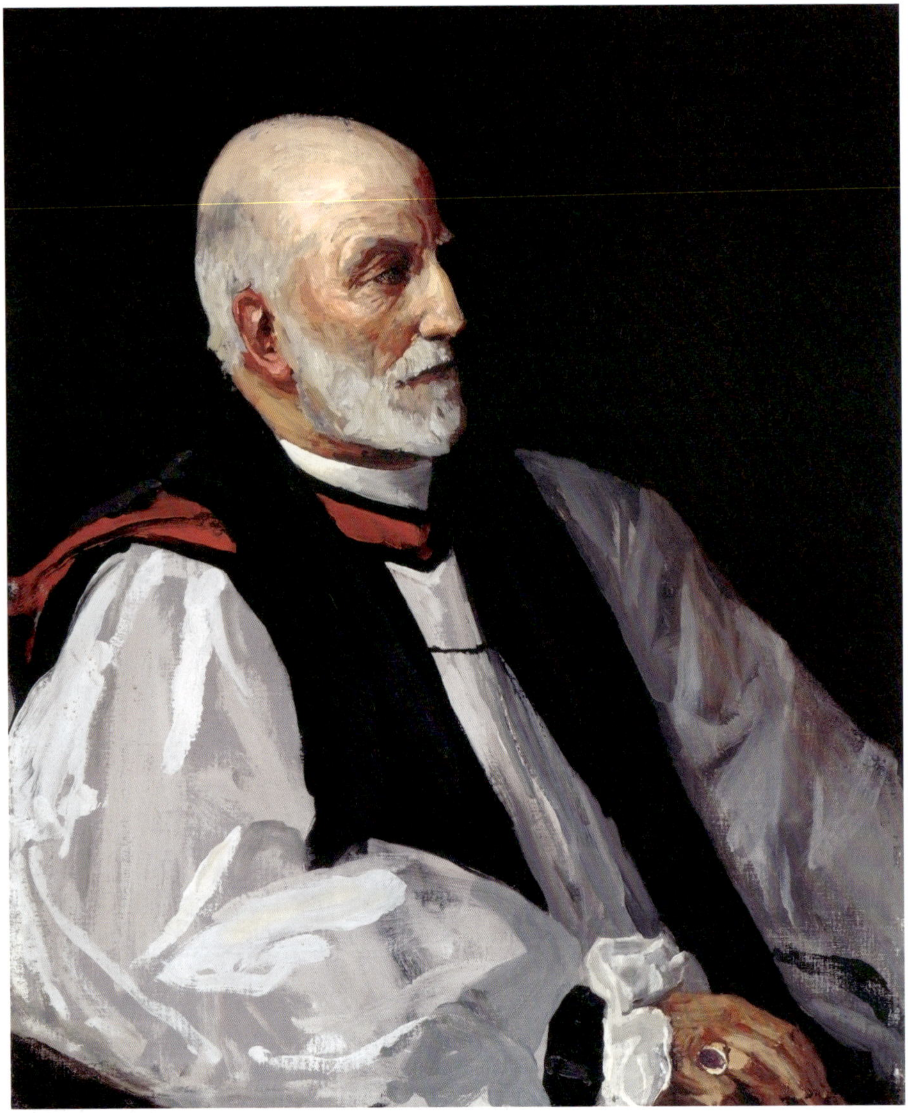

Rt. Rev. Dr. Charles T.P. Grierson 1857–1935, Bishop of Down and Dromore, 1928
Oil on canvas, 76.2 × 63.5 cm
Ulster Museum

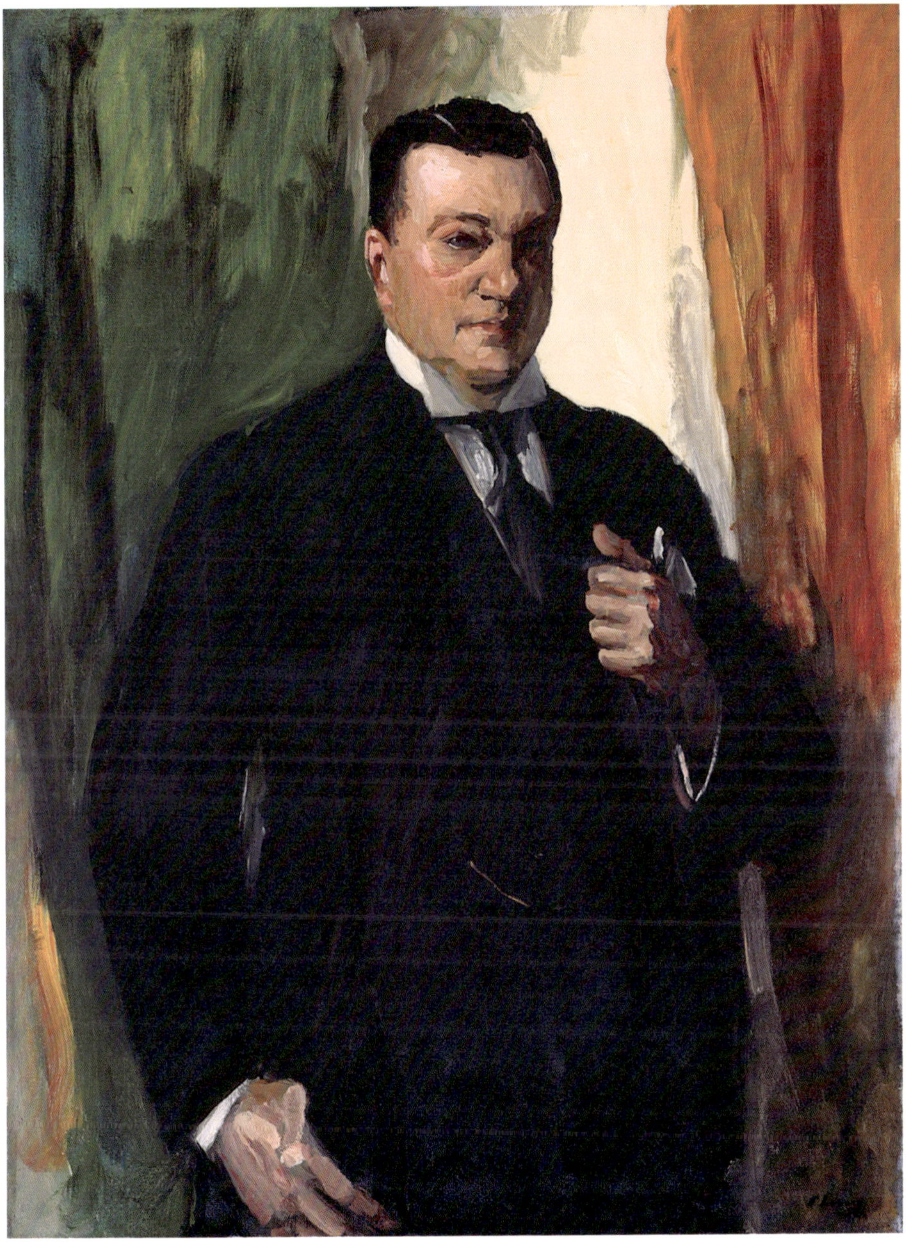

Joseph Devlin, MP *1871–1934,* 1928
Oil on canvas, 102.1 × 76.7 cm
Ulster Museum

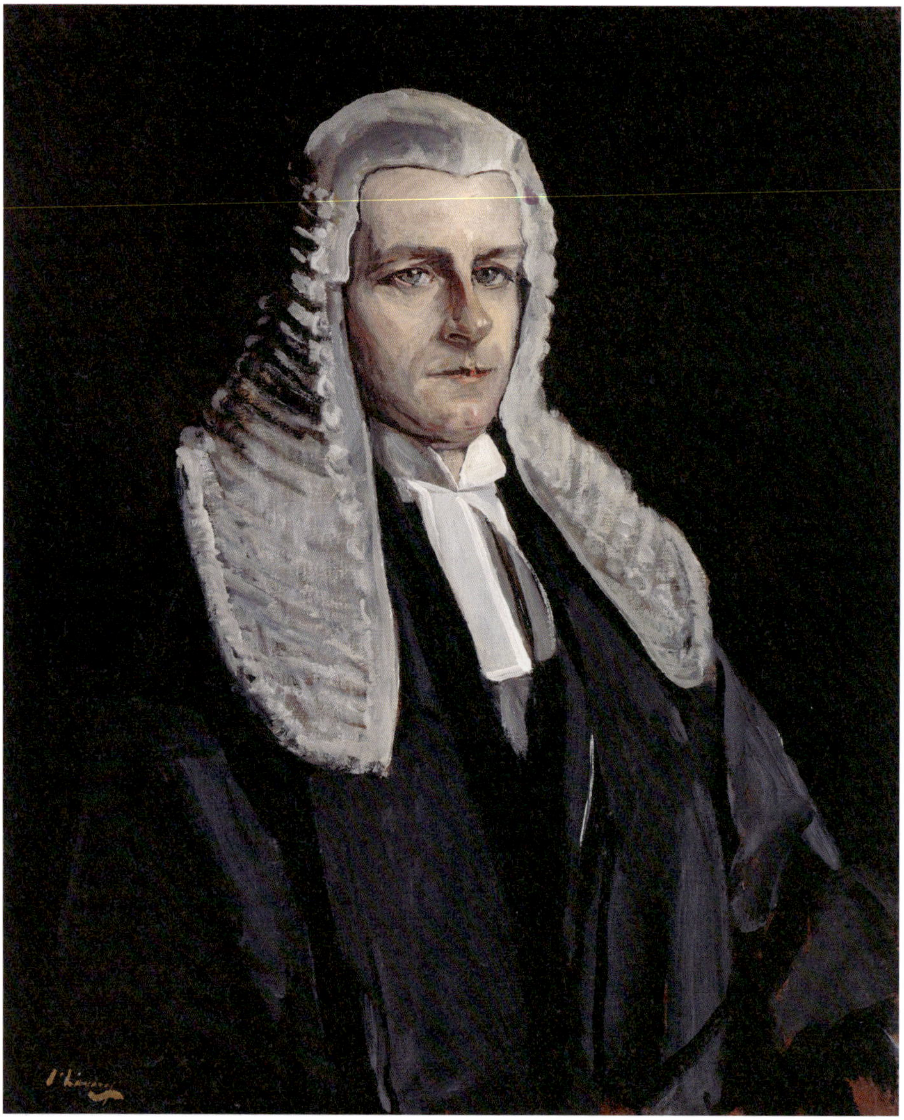

The Rt. Hon. Hugh O'Neill, PC, *First Speaker of the House of Commons, Northern Ireland,* 1922
Oil on canvas, 76.3 × 63.6 cm
Ulster Museum

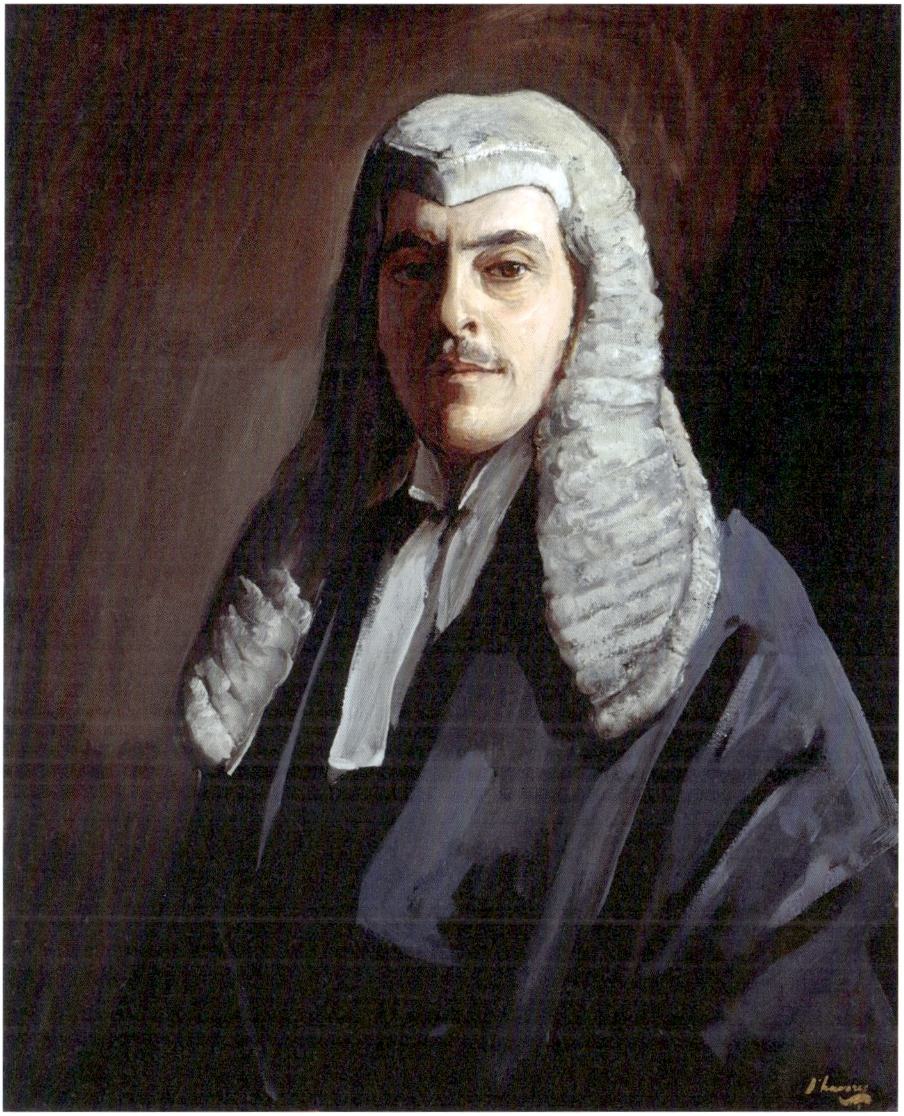

The Most Hon. the Marquis of Dufferin and Ava 1875–1930, First Speaker of the Senate, Northern Ireland, 1923
Oil on canvas, 76.2 × 63.5 cm
Ulster Museum

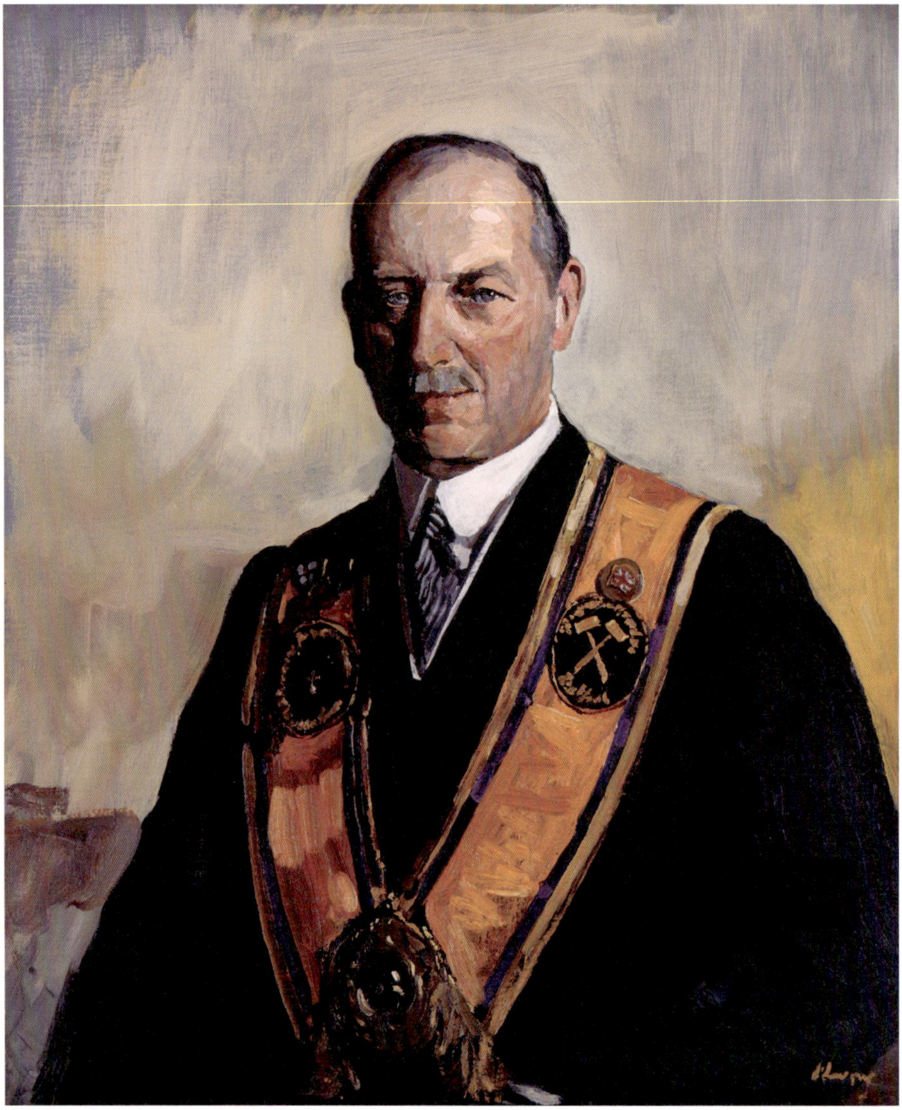

Sir Joseph Davison d. 1948, 1928
Oil on canvas, 76.1 × 63.7 cm
Ulster Museum

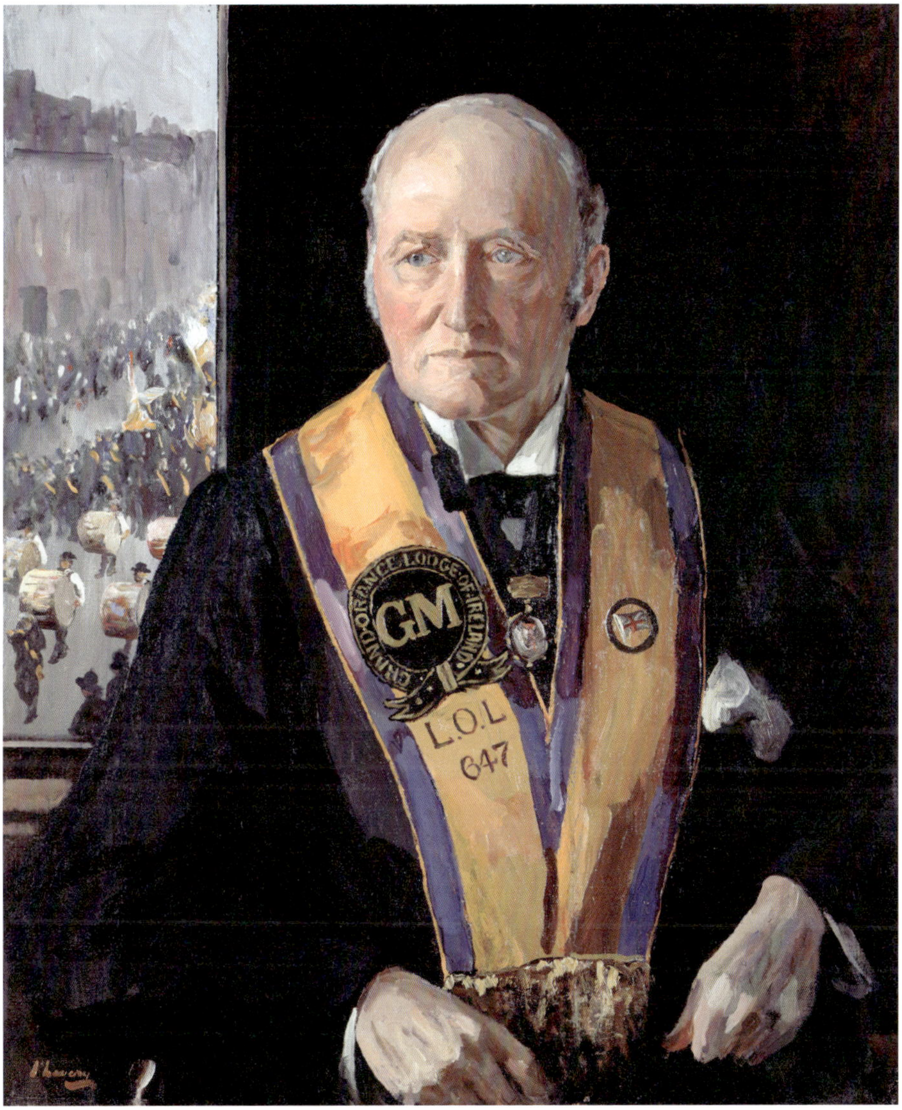

Sir Edward Mervyn Archdale, PC, DL *1853–1943*, 1928
Oil on canvas, 76.8 × 64.2 cm
Ulster Museum

the luxury of the Viceregal Lodge while Lavery painted this religious practice at Lough Derg.

In the summer of 1929 Hazel further alienated herself from Ireland when she appeared in an instructional film, *One Family*, produced for the British Empire Marketing Board.[190] In the film each Dominion was portrayed by a society lady. Hazel represented the Irish Free State, Lady Ravensdale represented New Zealand and Lady Zeeble represented Canada, while others depicted Australia and South Africa. The film script was written by J.M. Barrie, although this was not made public. It was shot in the Privy Council Chamber in Buckingham Palace, the first time that filming was allowed there. The story was of a young boy who meets a friendly policeman and together they go to the Palace where they are met by the 'Dominions', each of whom present the boy with a product from their country for his Christmas pudding. Hazel described herself as wearing a costume which was not in the slightest bit Gaelic in inspiration. The film was a 'talkie' and she wrote that she spoke in a 'rich Irish brogue'[191] and that Ireland's only contribution to the pudding seemed to be a basket of eggs. She described how an enormous wolf-hound kept following her around 'with embarrassing devotion and insisted upon throwing himself on my six yard train – you can imagine the difficulty of upholding Irish dignity under the circumstances.'[192]

In Belfast in September 1929 the new gallery opened with its special Lavery room. There were rumours that the Dublin paintings had been sent to Belfast. Negotiations continued behind the scenes, with Thomas Bodkin and President W.T. Cosgrave trying to resolve the issues that were impeding the acceptance of the gift to the National Gallery of Ireland.

The Laverys also lobbied for the return of Hugh Lane's paintings to Dublin.[193] Lady Gregory wrote to Hazel of her hopes that the issue of the return of the paintings would be raised in the House of Commons. Hazel's belief was that the English

189 Sir John Lavery had been suggested as MacNeill's successor as Governor General, but with the election of Eamon De Valera and his Fianna Fáil Party in 1932, it was a very different Ireland. MacNeill was dismissed and Donal Ui Buchalla was appointed in November 1932. He did not take up residence in Viceregal Lodge, opting to remain in his own home in Blackrock, Dublin. The new government policy was to break all constitutional links to Britain.

190 Lavery's granddaughter, Diana Dickinson, appeared in films such as *Frenchman's Creek* (1944) and *Titanic* (1953). Lavery loved to visited film studios. Despite his advanced years, he embraced this new world, visiting Hollywood in the late 1930s and painting the child actress, Shirley Temple (the work now in a private collection in the USA).

191 Hazel Lavery to Thomas Bodkin, 28 July 1929, quoted in McCoole, *Hazel*, p. 152.

192 Ibid.

193 Sir Hugh Lane had offered his collection of Modern French paintings to Dublin Corporation in exchange for the building of a gallery to house them. When this was not forthcoming, he removed the paintings to England. When he was appointed Director of the National Gallery, he had a change of heart and wrote a codicil to his will. He died on the *Lusitania* in 1914. The codicil was unwitnessed and a dispute over the return of the paintings went on for a number of years, led by his aunt, Augusta, Lady Gregory. She visited Lavery for the first time regarding this issue in December 1916.

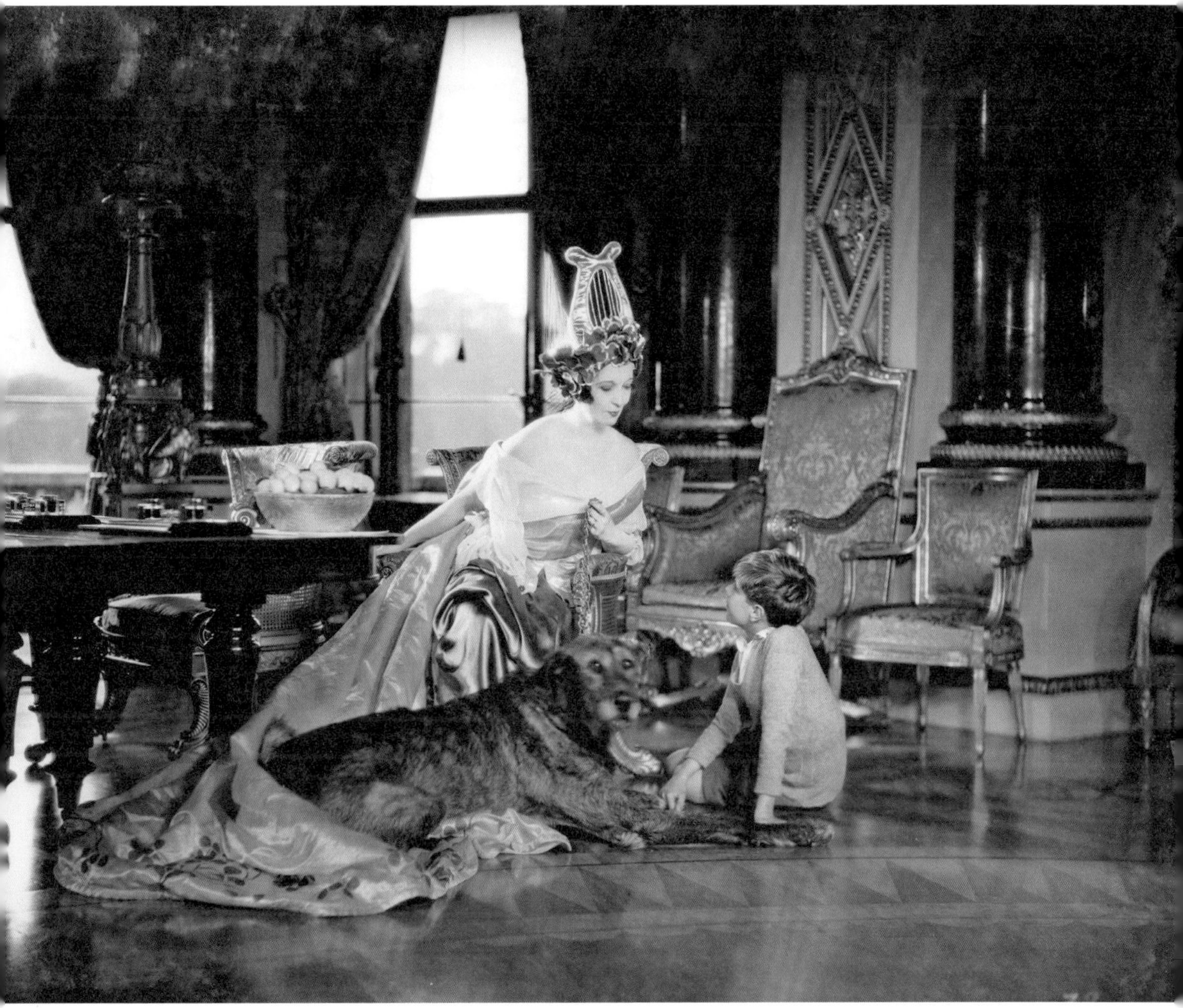

Lady Lavery representing the Irish Free State in *One Family*, British Instructional Films, 1930

BFI / COI

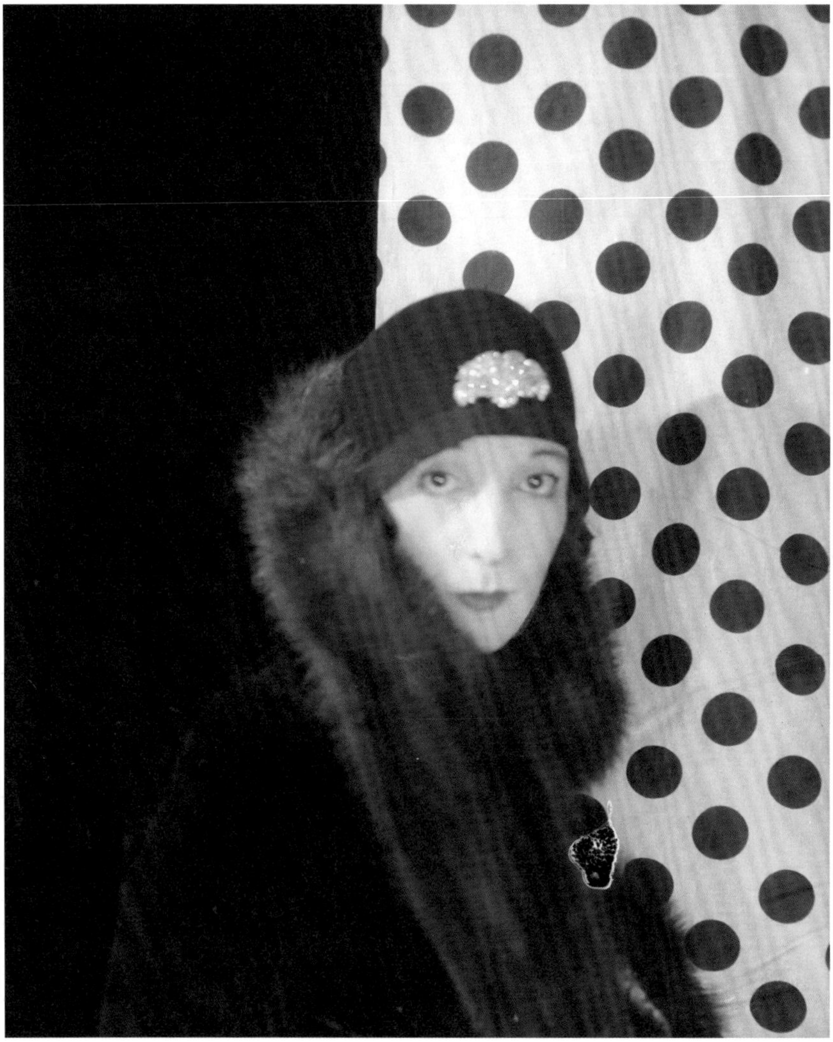

Cecil Beaton: *Lady Lavery*, c.1930

Courtesy of the Cecil Beaton Studio Archive at Sotheby's

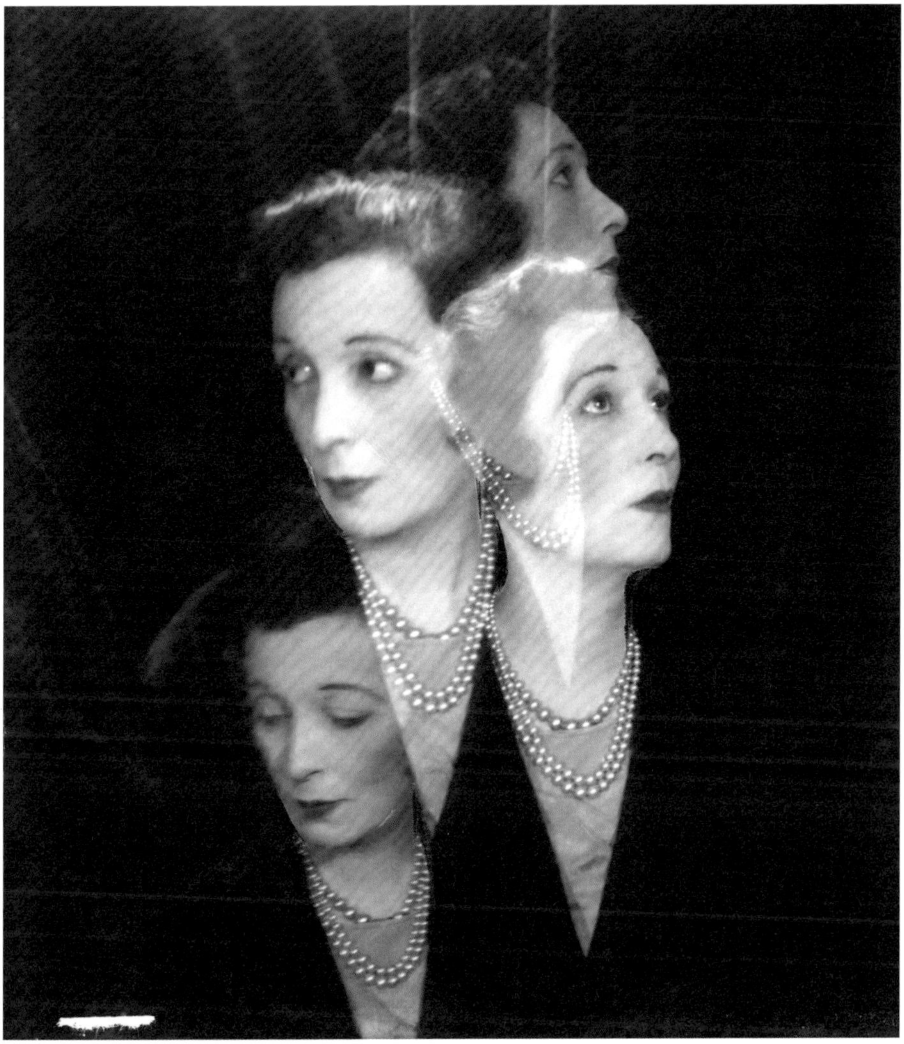

Cecil Beaton: *Lady Lavery*, c.1930
This photograph was reproduced in Cecil Beaton, *The Book of Beauty*, Duckworth, London, 1930.
Courtesy of the Cecil Beaton Studio Archive at Sotheby's

were 'not in a mood' to do flattering and generous gestures towards the Irish Free State, but, regardless, went to see the Prime Minister to keep the possibility of the return alive. She was a close confidante of Ramsay MacDonald who had become British Prime Minister.[194] This contact helped Hazel to continue lobbying for Irish issues during his tenure.[195]

Determined to maintain their lifestyle during times of economic difficulty in the late 1920s and early 1930s, the Laverys travelled to the south of France to paint wealthy visitors. They also made several extended visits to the US and painted portrait after portrait of American millionaires.[196] Lavery enjoyed America immensely. Hazel hated travelling there with him, however; it was 1925 before she made her first visit since Dorothy's death in 1911 and there is no record she ever returned to Chicago. When she finally returned to London in April 1926, she wrote: 'It is so wonderful to be home again, but I shall not really feel at home until I go to Ireland'. In truth she was happiest in London with her cult following of young men, the so-called 'Hazel Boys' – Brendan Bracken,[197] Douglas Woodruffe[198] and Randolph Churchill.[199] Evelyn Waugh was a frequent visitor to the house and he dedicated one of his books to her.[200] Romantic novelists used her as an inspiration for their characters, such as Temple Thurston's heroine Jane Carroll. Louie Rickard tried to capture Hazel's 'wonderful gay self' in her story, *A Bird of Strange Plumage*.[201] Cecil Beaton, too, was in her circle. She modelled for him, and he had used her images in his *Book of Beauty* and *Vogue* magazine.

They were still a celebrity couple. He was even selected as a 'popular personality' in a 1935 cigarette card collection. Like other society and titled ladies, Hazel took part in a Pond's Cold Cream advertisement, which featured her husband's famous portraits, *Hazel in Mauve and Rose* (now *The Green Coat*, 1925, Ulster Museum) and *The Silver Swan*, 1922 (Guildhall Art Gallery, London). MacDonald teased Hazel that if his portrait were so attractive he would 'use it for face cream too'.[202] The Laverys embraced

194 From 1929 to 1931 Ramsay McDonald was leader of the Labour Party in Britain, and from August 1931 to 1935 headed a National Government.

195 When Lavery presented his collection to the Municipal Gallery, he wrote to Mr Reynolds: 'I am much grateful and honoured by the Corporation having decided to defer to my wish that the collection should be shown in the Lane Room until such time as that collection, now in London, shall be placed here.' John Lavery to John Reynolds, 1 August 1935 (Dublin City Gallery The Hugh Lane Archive)

196 One newspaper stated that he painted forty American millionaires.

197 Brendan Bracken, from Templemore, County Tipperary, was a journalist and founder of the *Financial Times*. He was an MP from 1929 to 1945 and Minister for Information in Britain's wartime government; he was later given a title. The rumour that he was Churchill's illegitimate son was fuelled by Bracken himself.

198 Douglas Woodruffe was in later years editor of *The Tablet*, 1936–1967.

199 Winston Churchill's only son. He was a journalist and an MP. He was his father's first biographer

200 Evelyn Waugh dedicated *Remote People* to her and *When the Going was Good* was dedicated to her memory.

201 This book does not appear to have been published, perhaps because Alice was shocked by it and thought the heroine was a vampire. Hazel Lavery to Louie Rickard, 30 September 1927. See McCoole, *Hazel*, p. 161.

202 Ramsay MacDonald to Hazel Lavery, undated 1931, quoted in McCoole, *Hazel*, p. 170.

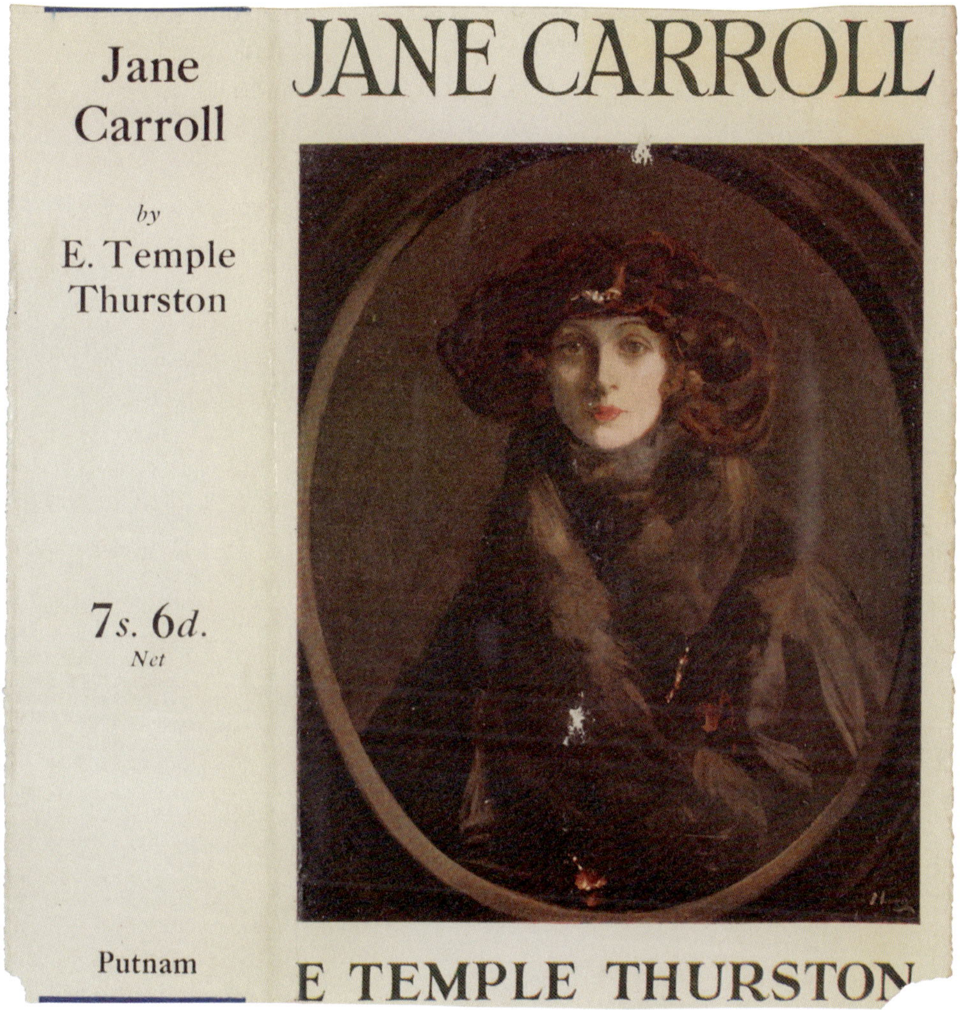

Dust jacket of E. Temple Thurston's *Jane Carroll* (1927)
with *Hazel Lavery (The Brown Furs / Dame en Noir)*, 1906

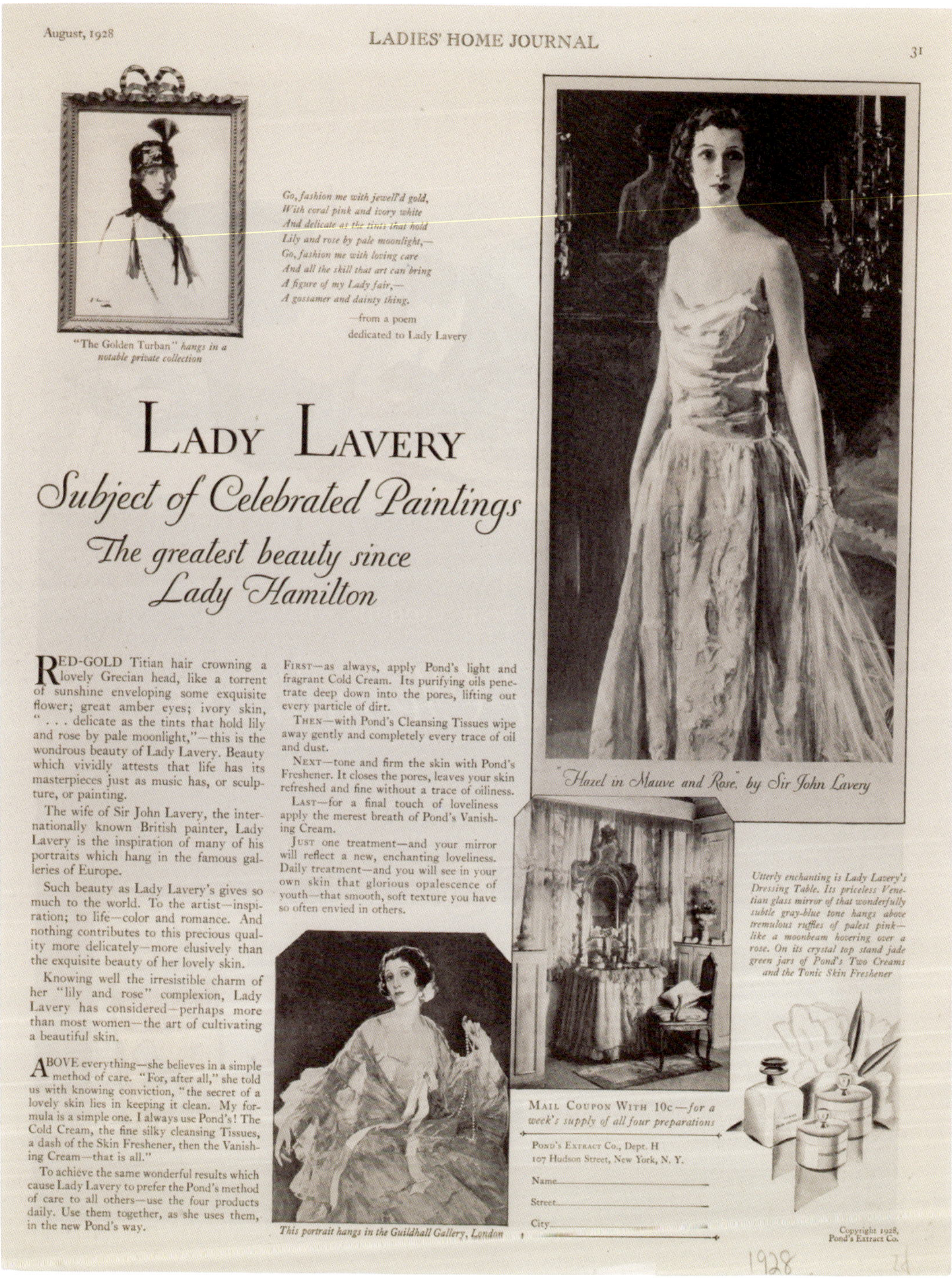

August, 1928 LADIES' HOME JOURNAL 31

"The Golden Turban" *hangs in a notable private collection*

Go, fashion me with jewell'd gold,
With coral pink and ivory white
And delicate as the tints that hold
Lily and rose by pale moonlight,—
Go, fashion me with loving care
And all the skill that art can bring
A figure of my Lady fair,—
A gossamer and dainty thing.

—from a poem dedicated to Lady Lavery

LADY LAVERY

Subject of Celebrated Paintings

The greatest beauty since Lady Hamilton

RED-GOLD Titian hair crowning a lovely Grecian head, like a torrent of sunshine enveloping some exquisite flower; great amber eyes; ivory skin, ". . . delicate as the tints that hold lily and rose by pale moonlight,"—this is the wondrous beauty of Lady Lavery. Beauty which vividly attests that life has its masterpieces just as music has, or sculpture, or painting.

The wife of Sir John Lavery, the internationally known British painter, Lady Lavery is the inspiration of many of his portraits which hang in the famous galleries of Europe.

Such beauty as Lady Lavery's gives so much to the world. To the artist—inspiration; to life—color and romance. And nothing contributes to this precious quality more delicately—more elusively than the exquisite beauty of her lovely skin.

Knowing well the irresistible charm of her "lily and rose" complexion, Lady Lavery has considered—perhaps more than most women—the art of cultivating a beautiful skin.

ABOVE everything—she believes in a simple method of care. "For, after all," she told us with knowing conviction, "the secret of a lovely skin lies in keeping it clean. My formula is a simple one. I always use Pond's! The Cold Cream, the fine silky cleansing Tissues, a dash of the Skin Freshener, then the Vanishing Cream—that is all."

To achieve the same wonderful results which cause Lady Lavery to prefer the Pond's method of care to all others—use the four products daily. Use them together, as she uses them, in the new Pond's way.

FIRST—as always, apply Pond's light and fragrant Cold Cream. Its purifying oils penetrate deep down into the pores, lifting out every particle of dirt.

THEN—with Pond's Cleansing Tissues wipe away gently and completely every trace of oil and dust.

NEXT—tone and firm the skin with Pond's Freshener. It closes the pores, leaves your skin refreshed and fine without a trace of oiliness.

LAST—for a final touch of loveliness apply the merest breath of Pond's Vanishing Cream.

JUST one treatment—and your mirror will reflect a new, enchanting loveliness. Daily treatment—and you will see in your own skin that glorious opalescence of youth—that smooth, soft texture you have so often envied in others.

This portrait hangs in the Guildhall Gallery, London

"Hazel in Mauve and Rose," by Sir John Lavery

Utterly enchanting is Lady Lavery's Dressing Table. Its priceless Venetian glass mirror of that wonderfully subtle gray-blue tone hangs above tremulous ruffles of palest pink—like a moonbeam hovering over a rose. On its crystal top stand jade green jars of Pond's Two Creams and the Tonic Skin Freshener

MAIL COUPON WITH 10c—*for a week's supply of all four preparations*

POND'S EXTRACT CO., Dept. H
107 Hudson Street, New York, N. Y.

Name____________
Street____________
City____________

Copyright 1928, Pond's Extract Co.

Pond's Advertisement featuring Lady Lavery,
Ladies Home Journal, August 1928

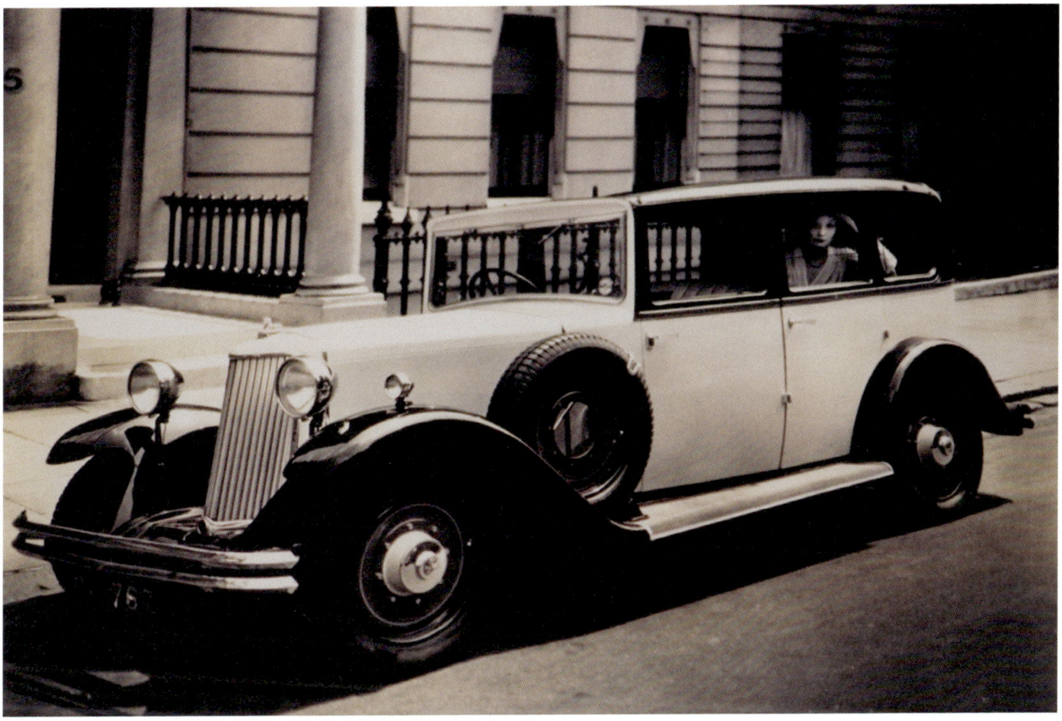

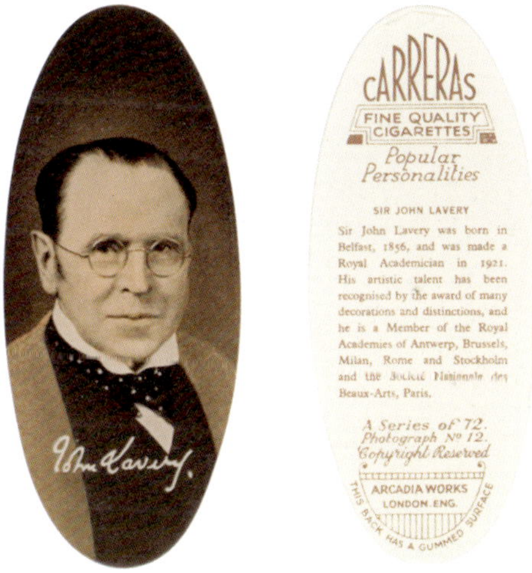

Hazel in an Armstrong Siddeley motorcar outside 5 Cromwell Place, London, 1932
Private collection

Carreras cigarette card featuring Sir John Lavery from the 'Popular Personalities' series, 1935

the new world of commercialism, entering the world of advertising by promoting Armstrong Siddeley Motors. In 1932 a coach-built saloon from Armstrong Siddeley Motors was loaned to 'the renowned artist and portrait painter' and his wife, a 'socialite and model'. In exchange for the use of the car, Armstrong Siddeley Motors did a series of posed photographs with the Laverys with the car outside Cromwell Place in May 1932.[203] The images were distributed to the motoring press.[204]

These years also brought Lavery many accolades. Lavery's success was international as a member of the academies of Rome, Paris, Berlin, Antwerp, Milan, Brussels, Stockholm and Spain, and his is paintings were in collections on five continents.[205] He was the first Catholic and the first artist to be awarded the Freedom of Belfast in 1930. He was awarded an honorary degree from Queen's University Belfast. He recorded the event in a self-portrait in which he wore his doctoral gown, with the silver casket which had been given to him depicted in the foreground. The painting, completed in 1935, today hangs in the Great Hall of Queen's University. He was also made a Freeman of Dublin in 1935 and given an honorary degree from Trinity College Dublin in 1936.

'Wee John Lavery' the orphan had painted monarchs, travelled extensively in his lifetime, including spending many of his final days in Hollywood. His canny approach to working at his career had brought him commercial success, recognition by his peers, clients and the wider artistic world and had gained him a world-wide reputation. When he died he left in his will £66,082 (approximately €2 million in today's money).[206] He lived a long and interesting public life. As he had himself revealed in his candid autobiography, *Life of a Painter* (1940), he had had a tragic personal life, outliving Kathleen, Hazel and his own daughter Eileen[207] who died of Tuberculosis in July 1935 just months after Hazel passed away, and his granddaughter June (one of Eileen's three daughters) who was killed by a bomb in the Second World War.

203 The car number is 66270. When the car was returned it was sold to the Countess of Antrim.

204 Bill Smith, *Armstrong Siddeley Motors, the Cars, the Company and the People*, Veloce Publishing, 2002, pp. 231–232.

205 Obituary, 1941, Scrapbook belonging to Alice McEnery (private collection).

206 *The Times*, 9 May 1941, p. 7. I am grateful to Paul Turnell for sourcing this for me.

207 Eileen, known as the Hon. Eileen Forbes-Sempill, had married the Hon. William Forbes-Sempill (later Lord Sempill) in 1920. Their daughter Ann was born that year. A second daughter, June, was born in 1922 in Japan, where Billy Sempill was heading the British Aviation Mission.

It was in the vivid visual diary of his life and times that he left his powerful legacy to the land of his birth. Lavery maintained that he merely painted what he saw rather than seeking to make a historical record: 'What age should an artist paint, if not his own? He sees about him men and things, and is moved to paint them.'[208] Yet, as McConkey has remarked, he had a 'paparazzi-like' intuition for what was the moment to paint.[209] Critics like Moya Llewelyn Davies, who with her husband Crompton assisted the Irish cause, wrote of them: 'I felt that both the Laverys were publicity hunters, running after the men of the moment, the one to paint, the other to embrace!'[210] When Lavery moved from commissioned work to his own choice of subject matter, he created images of the events and people who made history. W.B. Yeats recalled in a speech delivered at the banquet of the Irish Academy of Letters on 17 August 1937 that Sir John Lavery's work in the Municipal Gallery was: 'Ireland not as she is displayed in guide book or history, but Ireland seen because of the magnificent vitality of her painters in the glory of her passions'. [211]

As we approach the hundredth anniversary of the key events in Irish history through which the Laverys lived – the Rising, the First World War, the War of Independence, the Civil War, the foundation of the Irish Free State, the establishment of Northern Ireland – this exhibition itself is historic, as it brings both parts of Lavery's 'Island of Ireland' collection together for the first time.

208 'Sir John Lavery – His Works a Record of Modern Life,' *Sunday Times*, c.1930, Lady Lavery Scrapbooks (private collection).

209 Kenneth McConkey on 'Eye Candy' RTE Radio 1, first broadcast December 2003.

210 Moya Llewelyn Davies to P.S. O'Hegarty, 8 June 1943, (National Library of Ireland, MS 41,780).

211 'The Municipal Gallery Revisited', *Yeats Annual*, no.10, pp.160-161. I am grateful to Paddy Hawe for this reference.

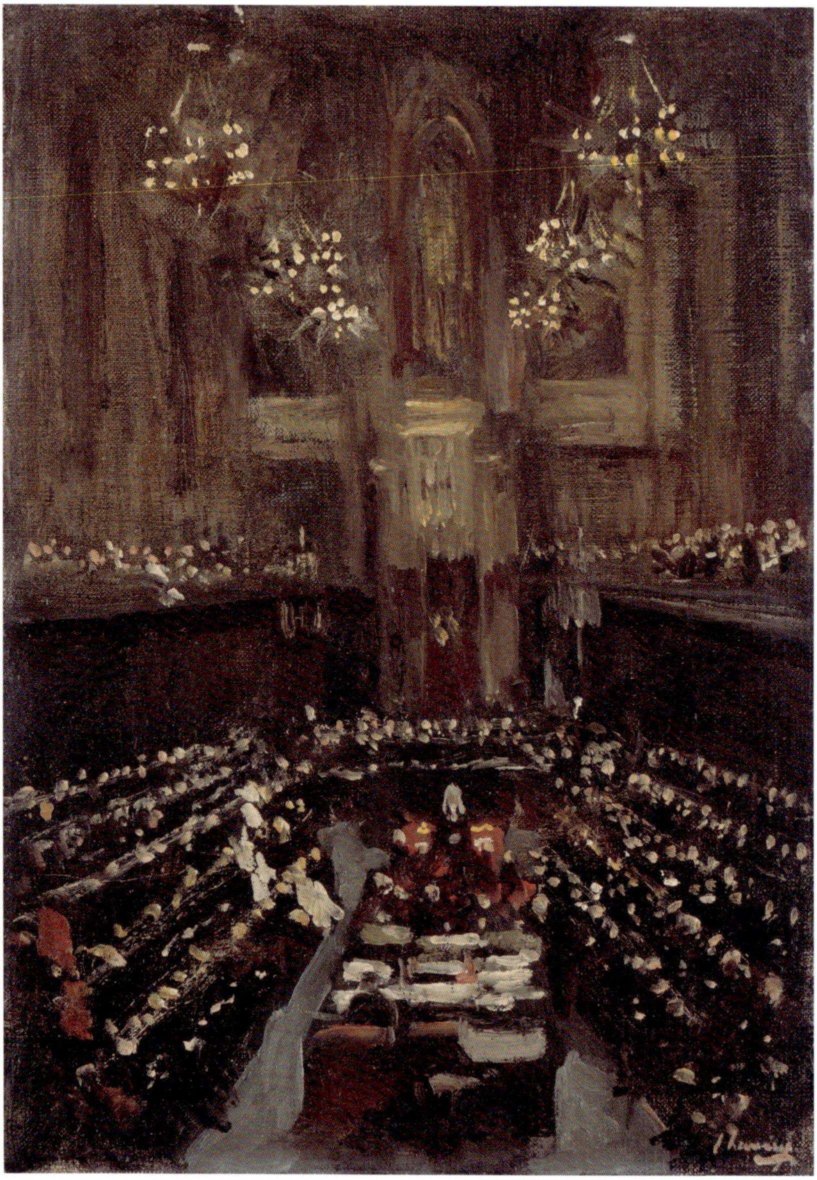

The Ratification of the Irish Treaty in the English House of Lords, 1921, 1921
Oil on board, 36 × 26 cm
Collection, National Gallery of Ireland

Paintings and Drawings in the Exhibition

Sir John Lavery (1856–1941)

Hazel Lavery (The Brown Furs / Dame en Noir)
1906
Oil on canvas, 77.2 × 64.5 cm
Collection Dublin City Gallery The Hugh Lane
Lady Lavery Memorial Bequest through
Sir John Lavery, 1935
p. 33

Self-portrait
1909
Oil on canvas, 68.5 × 61 cm
Kilkenny Archaeological Society, Rothe House, Kilkenny
Donated to the Society by Alice Gwynn, 1986
p. 25

Mrs Lavery Sketching
1910
Oil on canvas, 203.2 × 99 cm
Collection Dublin City Gallery The Hugh Lane
Presented by Hugh Lane, 19104
p. 34

Japanese Switzerland
1913
Oil on board, 76.1 × 53.3 cm
Dublin City Gallery The Hugh Lane Loan Collection
p. 49

Second Study for the King, the Queen, the Prince of Wales, the Princess Mary, Buckingham Palace
1913
Oil on canvas, 76.1 × 63.4 cm
Ulster Museum
Donated by the artist, 1919
p. 44

Sir Winston Churchill
1915
Oil on canvas, 76.8 × 63.9 cm
Collection Dublin City Gallery The Hugh Lane
Lady Lavery Memorial Bequest through
Sir John Lavery, 1935
p. 73

John E. Redmond, MP
1916
Oil on canvas, 76.2 × 63.6 cm
Collection Dublin City Gallery The Hugh Lane
Presented by Lieutenant-Colonel Sir William Hutcheson-Poë in remembrance of Sir Hugh Lane, 1917
p. 65

Sir Edward Carson, MP
1916
Oil on canvas, 76.2 × 63.6 cm
Collection Dublin City Gallery The Hugh Lane
Presented by Lieutenant-Colonel Sir William Hutcheson-Poë in remembrance of Sir Hugh Lane, 1917
p. 64

The Court of Criminal Appeal. The Trial of Sir Roger Casement, London, 1916
1916
Oil on panel, 80 × 63.5 cm
Collection Dublin City Gallery The Hugh Lane
Lady Lavery Memorial Bequest through
Sir John Lavery, 1935
p. 68

High Treason, Court of Criminal Appeal: the Trial of Sir Roger Casement
1916
Oil on canvas, 194.5 × 302.5 cm
Government Art Collection, London
Bequeathed by the artist, 1941
p. 69

The Madonna of the Lakes
1917
Oil on canvas, triptych: 277 × 385 cm (framed)
The Parish of St Patrick, Belfast
pp. 58–59

Southwark Cathedral, London, 1920 (Terence MacSwiney)
1920
Oil on canvas, 99 × 134.6 cm
Collection Dublin City Gallery The Hugh Lane
Lady Lavery Memorial Bequest through
Sir John Lavery, 1935
p. 75

Michael Collins (with his 'moustache' disguise)
1921
Lithograph, published by Wilson Hartnell & Co., Dublin, 51 × 41 cm
Jackie Clarke Library and Archive, Ballina
p. 84

Arthur Griffith
1921
Oil on canvas, 76.9 × 63.9 cm
Collection Dublin City Gallery The Hugh Lane
Lady Lavery Memorial Bequest through
Sir John Lavery, 1935
p. 78

Eamon J. Duggan
1921
Oil on canvas, 76.8 × 64.6 cm
Collection Dublin City Gallery The Hugh Lane
Lady Lavery Memorial Bequest through
Sir John Lavery, 1935

Robert Barton
1921
Oil on canvas, 76.2 × 63.6 cm
Collection Dublin City Gallery The Hugh Lane
Lady Lavery Memorial Bequest through
Sir John Lavery, 1935

George Gavan Duffy
1921
Oil on canvas, 76.2 × 63.5 cm
Collection Dublin City Gallery The Hugh Lane
Lady Lavery Memorial Bequest through
Sir John Lavery, 1935

Sir Austin Chamberlain
1921
Oil on board, 75.9 × 63.3 cm
Collection Dublin City Gallery The Hugh Lane
Lady Lavery Memorial Bequest through
Sir John Lavery, 1935

Eamon De Valera
1921
Oil on canvas, 91.5 × 71.1 cm
Collection Dublin City Gallery The Hugh Lane
Lady Lavery Memorial Bequest through
Sir John Lavery, 1935

The Ratification of the Irish Treaty in the English House of Lords, 1921
1921
Oil on board, 36 × 26 cm
Collection, National Gallery of Ireland
Purchased, 1963
p. 118

The Blessing of the Colours
1922
Oil on canvas, 243.8 × 182.9 cm
Collection Dublin City Gallery The Hugh Lane
Lady Lavery Memorial Bequest through
Sir John Lavery, 1935
p. 81

Timothy Healy
1922
Oil on canvas, 89.5 × 71.1 cm
Collection Dublin City Gallery The Hugh Lane
Lady Lavery Memorial Bequest through
Sir John Lavery, 1935

David Lloyd George
1922
Oil on canvas, 76.2 × 63.6 cm
Collection Dublin City Gallery The Hugh Lane
Lady Lavery Memorial Bequest through
Sir John Lavery, 1935

Major Compton Smith
1922
Oil on canvas, 61 × 50.8 cm
Collection Dublin City Gallery The Hugh Lane
Lady Lavery Memorial Bequest through
Sir John Lavery, 1935

Michael Collins (Love of Ireland)
1922
Oil on canvas, 63.8 × 76.8 cm
Collection Dublin City Gallery The Hugh Lane
Lady Lavery Memorial Bequest through
Sir John Lavery, 1935
p. 87

Chief Justice Hugh Kennedy
1922
Oil on canvas, 76.2 × 63.5 cm
Collection Dublin City Gallery The Hugh Lane
Lady Lavery Memorial Bequest through
Sir John Lavery, 1935

Pro-Cathedral, Dublin, 1922 (Michael Collins)
1922
Oil on canvas, 125.7 × 100.3 cm
Collection Dublin City Gallery The Hugh Lane
Lady Lavery Memorial Bequest through
Sir John Lavery, 1935
p. 88

The Rt. Hon. Hugh O'Neill, PC, First Speaker of the House of Commons, Northern Ireland
1922
Oil on canvas, 76.3 × 63.6 cm
Ulster Museum
Donated by the artist, 1929
p. 104

Lord Carson, PC *1854–1935*
1922
Oil on canvas, 91.4 × 71.1 cm
Ulster Museum
Donated by the artist, 1929

The Earl of Birkenhead
1923
Oil on canvas, 76.2 × 63.6 cm
Collection Dublin City Gallery The Hugh Lane
Lady Lavery Memorial Bequest through
Sir John Lavery, 1935

William Cosgrave
1923
Oil on canvas, 91.5 × 71.1 cm
Collection Dublin City Gallery The Hugh Lane
Lady Lavery Memorial Bequest through
Sir John Lavery, 1935

Kevin O'Higgins
1923
Oil on board, 101.6 × 76.2 cm
Collection Dublin City Gallery The Hugh Lane
Lady Lavery Memorial Bequest through
Sir John Lavery, 1935
p. 79

Rt. Hon. The Viscount Craigavon 1871–1940, First Prime Minister of Northern Ireland
1923
Oil on canvas, 91.5 × 71.1 cm
Ulster Museum
Donated by the artist, 1929
p. 90

The Most Hon. the Marquis of Dufferin and Ava 1875–1930, First Speaker of the Senate, Northern Ireland
1923
Oil on canvas, 76.2 × 63.5 cm
Ulster Museum
Donated by the artist, 1929
p. 105

The Marquess of Londonderry, KG *1878–1949, Chancellor of The Queen's University of Belfast*
c. 1924
Oil on canvas, 101.6 × 76.2 cm
Ulster Museum
Donated by the artist, 1929
p. 100

Sir Alfred Cope
1925
Oil on canvas, 71.4 × 54.7 cm
Collection Dublin City Gallery The Hugh Lane
Lady Lavery Memorial Bequest through
Sir John Lavery, 1935
p. 91

Portrait of Lady Lavery as Kathleen Ni Houlihan
1927
Oil on canvas, 75.5 × 62.5 cm
Collection, Central Bank & Financial Services
Authority of Ireland
p. 97

Most Rev. Charles Frederick D'Arcy, MA, DD *1859–1938, Archbishop of Armagh and Primate of All Ireland*
1928
Oil on canvas, 102.1 × 76.3 cm
Ulster Museum
Donated by the artist, 1929
p. 4

Joseph MacRory, DD 1861–1945, Archiepisciopus Armachanus Totius Hiberniae Primus
1928
Oil on canvas, 102.2 × 76.5 cm
Ulster Museum
Donated by the artist, 1929
p.7

Joseph Devlin, MP 1871–1934
1928
Oil on canvas, 102.1 × 76.7 cm
Ulster Museum
Donated by the artist, 1929
p.103

Sir Edward Mervyn Archdale, PC, DL 1853–1943
1928
Oil on canvas, 76.8 × 64.2 cm
Ulster Museum
Donated by the artist, 1929
p.107

Sir Joseph Davison d. 1948
1928
Oil on canvas, 76.1 × 63.7 cm
Ulster Museum
Donated by the artist, 1929
p.106

The Twelfth of July in Portadown
1928
Oil on board, 63.8 × 76.4 cm
Ulster Museum
Donated by the artist, 1929

Self-portrait
1928
Oil on canvas, 107.6 × 77 cm
Ulster Museum
Donated by the artist, 1929

Rt. Rev. Dr. Charles T.P. Grierson 1857–1935, Bishop of Down and Dromore
1928
Oil on canvas, 76.2 × 63.5 cm
Ulster Museum
Donated by the artist, 1929
p.102

St Patrick's Purgatory
1930
Oil on canvas, 58.5 × 106.5 cm
Collection Dublin City Gallery The Hugh Lane
Lady Lavery Memorial Bequest through
Sir John Lavery, 1936

Michael Collins
c. 1935
Oil on canvas, 63.8 × 76.8 cm
Collection Dublin City Gallery The Hugh Lane
Lady Lavery Memorial Bequest through
Sir John Lavery, 1935

'It is Finished'. 5th January 1935 (Lady Lavery)
1935
Oil on canvas board, 50.8 × 60.4 cm
Collection Dublin City Gallery The Hugh Lane
Lady Lavery Memorial Bequest through
Sir John Lavery, 1935

Self-portrait
1935
Oil on canvas, 101.5 × 76.3 cm (framed)
Collection of Queen's University, Belfast
p. 2

Lady Lavery in an Evening Cloak
c. 1918 or c. 1935
Oil on canvas, 46 × 36 cm
Collection, National Gallery of Ireland
Presented by the Executors of the late Mr. E. Marsh, 1953

Lady Hazel Lavery (1880–1935)

Portrait of a Young Girl
1903
Oil on canvas, 51 × 41 cm
Private collection
p. 27

Harrington Mann (1864–1937)

Portrait of Alice Gwynn-Lavery
1910
Oil on canvas, 61 × 45.7 cm
Kilkenny Archaeological Society, Rothe House, Kilkenny
Donated to the Society by Alice Gwynn, 1986

John Singer Sargent (1856–1925)

Lady Hazel Lavery (c. 1887–1935), 2nd Wife of the Artist, Sir John Lavery
1923
Charcoal on paper, 60 × 47 cm
Collection, National Gallery of Ireland
Presented by Mrs. A. Gwynn, 1982
p. 92

David Wilson (1873–1935)

Sir John Lavery R.A.
c. 1912
Ink on paper, 35.1 × 26 cm
Collection Dublin City Gallery The Hugh Lane
Presented by Joseph Holloway, 1943
p. 28

No 1020 KENSINGTON.

5, CROMWELL PLACE,
S.W.7.

LIST OF PICTURES PRESENTED AS A FREE GIFT TO THE CITY OF DUBLIN

IN MEMORY OF LADY LAVERY BY HER HUSBAND.

****

1. John Lavery by Hazel Lavery.
2. Timothy O'Healy.
3. Arthur Griffith.
4. Michael Collins.
5. E.S.O.Duggan.
6. Robert Barton.
7. Gavan Duffy.
8. David Lloyd George.
9. The Earl of Birkenhead.
10. Winston Churchill.
11. Sir Austen Chamberlain.
12. Major Compton Smith (Posthumous).
13. William Cosgrave.
14. Archbishop Mannix.
15. Kevin O'Higgins.
16. Eamon de Valera.
17. Michael Collins (Love of Ireland)
18. Hugh Nihill Kennedy.
19. Sir Horace Plunket.
20. The Earl of Dunraven.
21. Viscount Northcliffe.
22. George Bernard Shaw.
23. Shane Leslie.
24. Pro Cathedral.........Dublin 1922.
25. Southwark Cathedral....London 1920.
26. Court of Criminal Appeal.....London 1916.
27. The First Irish Air-Woman.
28. Air Alfred Cope.
29. The Blessing of the Colours. — *already used, 1933*
30. Count John MacCormack and his Family.
31. Hazel Lavery by John Lavery.
32. St. Patrick's Purgatory.
33. The Unfinished Harmony. 1934.
34. It is Finished. 4th. January 1935.

****

Typescript list of 'Pictures presented as a free gift to the city of Dublin in memory of Lady Lavery by her husband', accompanying letter from Sir John Lavery to John Reynolds, curator, Municipal Gallery of Modern Art, 13 August 1935
Dublin City Gallery The Hugh Lane Archive

Bibliography

Sir John Lavery, *Life of a Painter*, London, 1940.

Sinéad Nic Cumhaill, *Lady Lavery, Her Salon and its Role in the Emergence of the Irish Free State*, University College Dublin, 1991.

Kenneth McConkey, *Sir John Lavery*, Canongate Press, Edinburgh, 1993.

Kenneth McConkey, *Sir John Lavery, a Painter and his World*, Atelier Books, Edinburgh, 2010.

Sinead McCoole, *Hazel: A Life of Lady Lavery, 1880–1935*, The Lilliput Press, Dublin, 1996.

Lady Audrey Morris, Unpublished manuscript on Lady Lavery, private collection.

Ian Chant Sempill, Unpublished manuscript on the Sempill family, private collection.

Walter Shaw Sparrow, *John Lavery & His Work*, London, 1911.

Acknowledgements

Sir John Lavery: Passion and Politics
Dublin City Gallery The Hugh Lane
15 July to 31 October 2010

Curated by Sinéad McCoole
Assisted by Michael Dempsey

Dublin City Gallery The Hugh Lane team for *Sir John Lavery: Passion and Politics*: Jessica O'Donnell, Logan Sisley, Katy Fitzpatrick, Rebecca Vodehnal, Carol Lyons, Mariana Centeno, Joanna Shepard, Liz Forster, Peadar Nolan, Mary Keogh, Eleanora Conti, Tim Haier, and all attendant staff.

Dublin City Gallery The Hugh Lane wishes to thank: Sinéad McCoole, guest curator; the individuals and institutions that have so generously lent their works to this exhibition: The Ulster Museum / National Museums Northern Ireland, Belfast, The National Gallery of Ireland, Dublin, The National Library of Ireland, Dublin, The Hoppé Estate Collection, Pasadena, CA, Kilkenny Archaeological Society, Rothe House, Kilkenny, Kilmainham Gaol Museum, Dublin, The UK Government Art Collection, London, The Parish of St Patrick, Belfast, The Jackie Clarke Archive and Library, Ballina, Queen's University Belfast, The British Film Institute, London, Trinity College Library, Dublin, British Pathé, and those lenders who wish to remain anonymous; and the following institutions and individuals who in various ways have helped to bring this exhibition and publication together: The Central Bank and Financial Services Authority of Ireland, Pym's Gallery, London, The National Portrait Gallery, London, Sarah Dotson, Prof. Giovanna Giusti, Graham Howe, Camilla McAleese, Kenneth McConkey, Eamon Manning, Colette O'Daly, Dairne O'Sullivan, Anna Patrick, Terence Pepper, Jamie and Josephine Sempill, Ian Chant Sempill, Father Michael Sheehan, Anne Stewart, Alex Sklrilis, and Elenei Tsopotou.

Author's acknowledgements

I am very grateful to Barbara Dawson, Director of Dublin City Gallery The Hugh Lane for this opportunity to revisit the Laverys. Thank you to her wonderful staff, Michael Dempsey, Jessica O'Donnell, Logan Sisley, Liz Forster, Katy Fitzpatrick, and Mary Keogh, for their advice and support: I wish to acknowledge Carla Briggs, Terry Browne, Valerie Butler, Anne Clarke, Ivan Clenaghan, Eleanora Conti, Dorothy Davison, Marion Flannery, Lori Gallagher, Paddy Hawe, Graham Howe, Christina Kennedy, Kenneth McConkey, Barbara McCoole, Fiona McCoole, Harry McKillop, Fr Brian Murphy, Loretta Clarke Murray, Colette O'Daly, Dairne O'Sullivan, Niamh O'Sullivan, Terence Pepper, Ian Chant Sempill, Jamie and Josephine Sempill, Joe Talbot, Ned and Patricia Trudeau, Paul Turnell, Austin Vaughan and Vincent Virga. Also to my family Eamon, Eve and Edward Howlin. And the final word of thanks to late Alice Gwynn and her descendants and to Dr. Margaret MacCurtain for giving me the encouragement at the start of my Lavery journey.

Published by Dublin City Gallery The Hugh Lane on the occasion of the exhibition, *Sir John Lavery: Passion and Politics*, 15 July to 31 October 2010.

Front cover: £100 Banknote (A Series), 4·4·77
Back cover: *Sir Edward Carson, MP*, 1916 and *John E. Redmond, MP*, 1916 (detail), Collection Dublin City Gallery The Hugh Lane

Editor: Logan Sisley
Copy editor: Elizabeth Mayes
Book design: Tony Waddingham
Printing: Cassochrome, Belgium

ISBN 978–1–901702–35–4

Dublin City Gallery The Hugh Lane
Charlemont House, Parnell Square North, Dublin 1
T: +353 222 5550
www.hughlane.ie

HUGH LANE dublin

Dublin City
Baile Átha Cliath

Supported by:

Fáilte Ireland
National Tourism Development Authority

THE IRISH TIMES

An Roinn
Turasóireachta, Cultúir agus Spóirt
Department of
Tourism, Culture and Sport